C000262039

MEMORIES
of Darlington

Cover design by Mike Brough
Illustrations by Petra Stanton

Published by The Northern Echo, Priestgate, Darlington, Co. Durham DL1 1NF
ISBN 0 9515288 5 8 Memories of Darlington (pbk)
© The Northern Echo

Contents

Acknowledgements

Chris Lloyd was born on November 23 1964 in Rush Green Hospital. This used to be in Dagenham but seems now to have moved into Romford. His family moved to St Ippolyts just outside Hitchin, Hertfordshire, when he was two. He attended the village school, where his dad was headmaster, then Hitchin Boys' School. In 1984 he went to the University of St Andrews where he gained a Master of Arts with Honours in English Language and Literature. He first came to Darlington in 1987 for an interview as a trainee journalist and, three days before Christmas of that year, began work on the Darlington and Stockton Times. Ten months later he was moved into the Darlington office of The Northern Echo where he became a qualified journalist in 1989 – picking up an award as one of the top six trainees in the country that year. He is now an established features writer on the paper.

Thanks to: Alyson Herbert and her staff at the Centre for Local Studies, Darlington whose patience and perserverance will hopefully be rewarded in heaven because never say thank you; Stan Dean for checking the manuscript and anyone who eve read, wrote or called.

Chris Lloy

Photographs

Present day pictures for Darlington Now and Then
Mel Attrill

All others by permission of Durham County Council,
Arts, Libraries and Museums Department

Introduction

ON September 26 1917, the manager of The Northern Echo Printing Department wrote to HG Steavenson, Darlington Town Clerk.

'Dear Sir,
We are proposing to issue, in accordance with the express desire of many towns-people, a book dealing with the Historical Associations of Darlington. This book will be profusely illustrated with the photographs of past and present councillors and with reproduction of many pictures.
The enormous cost of material, in some instances four or five times in excess of pre-war prices, will make the cost much heavier than in normal times, yet it does not seem to be wise to delay publication on this account. In bringing out this book we shall be risking a very considerable sum, but we suggest that it will be an invaluable work for schools for all time and we shall be prepared to publish a special edition as per attached proof, up to 3,000 copies at 2/- per copy; in green cloth at 3/- per copy. The books will also be invaluable to send out as advertising the Town's Industries. We shall also publish an edition de luxe bound in leather at half-a-guinea and to supply any of these copies that may be required for the Council.'

The book was to commemorate the 50th anniversary of Queen Victoria granting Darlington's Royal Charter of Incorporation on September 13 1867 and once again The Northern Echo is venturing into the realm of historical publications. The chapters of this book are a selection from The Northern Echo's regular feature, Extra Memories. The feature began in 1988 when the then editor Allan Prosser decided to devote more pages to Darlington. I was chosen to take responsibility for Extra Memories because I was in charge of a feature called Then and Now which consisted of a photograph taken way back and one taken more recently, plus a couple of choice sentences: 'The black cat crossing this road all those many years ago is probably long since dead and the baby in the pram has probably grown up into a bus driver with a family all of his own. When do you think the picture on the left was taken?' The last sentence often meant that I didn't have a clue but readers were swift to furnish me with the facts. Since then Extra Memories and its spin-offs Ghost of the Week and Tales from the Riverbank have become one of the most popular features in the paper.

If I make a mistake, and I admit to the odd one, the readers are always quick to correct it. One particular howler elicited 52 calls in the first hour. I was off that day so some-one else had to answer the phone but there were still 41 letters awaiting my return. I am confident, not least because of the efforts of Durham's former county librarian Stan Dean, there will be no such errors in this book. However, Extra Memories has never set out to be a definitive history of Darlington. It has always been far more concerned with the people and the anecdotes. Essentially it is about entertainment. I hope you enjoy the book.

Chris Lloyd

──── Now and Then ────
A pictorial stroll down Darlington's Memory Lane

Above: Bondgate horsemarket in the 1900s. Below: Bondgate today

Above: Northgate in 1905 with the Theatre Royal on the left and as it is now with the Cannon, the town's one remaining cinema, in its place

Geese on their way to market through Prospect Place at the turn of the century
Below: Looking from the same viewpoint in the 1990s

An elegant run of houses in Victoria Road in the early part of the century.
They were demolished to make way for the ring road, below

Transport from a bygone age. A horsedrawn tram at the top of Woodland Road on the way into Cockerton. The same place today, below, with cars and bike instead

Cockerton in 1963. The house on the right was demolished and its grounds built on to become the shopping centre and Strikes

Northgate before the ring road. Pictured in 1963 when it was a continuous shopping street. Below: As it is today looking towards Northgate House and the roundabout.

The ring road under construction in Northgate in 1972. The power station cooling towers in the background were demolished in 1978. Below: The view from the same spot today

Above: The Theatre Royal in Northgate pictured in 1937.
Below: The Hippodrome in Parkgate where the Civic Theatre is now

The Theatre

At the start of the Nineties, Darlington's only theatre, the Civic, is one of the most successful in the country – although staging plays and variety performances in the town has historically been a financially perilous venture. The earliest recorded performance in Darlington was in June 1768, probably in a field on the outskirts of town, although it is likely that medieval morality plays were performed in churchyards.

One of the first theatres was a wooden building in a field near Clay Row. It was built in the early 19th Century and had an open air stage. It was called Thorn's Theatre and in the 1840s moved to a yard on the north side of Blackwellgate and became known as the Albert Saloon. In the late 1840s a large crowd gathered to see a Shakespearean play. They became so excited at King Richard's offer of his kingdom for a horse that the gallery collapsed injuring many. The Albert Saloon never reopened. The Barn Theatre took over in 1858. It was another wooden building in a field behind Skinnergate. Shakespeare was keenly performed, but the influential Quakers regarded such entertainment as morally corrupt. In 1859 mill-owners Henry Pease and Co issued a notice to all employees. It read:

The evils resulting from the attendances of Theatres are so great, and so well known, that it is with much concern we learn that a license has again been granted for opening a Theatre in Darlington, contrary to the known wishes of those who are, year by year, bestowing their time and means in promoting every effort that has for its object your temporal, moral and religious elevation.
We ask you then – as you value the confidence of your employers, your health, your character, your claim to the title of Christians – never to go within the doors of a Theatre.

The advice went unheeded and the Barn became so popular that it adopted the name Royal. On March 21, 1861, the new Theatre Royal gave a performance to raise funds to mount the Crimean War gun in

South Park. The first purpose-built playhouse in Darlington was in Northgate where the Cannon cinema is now. Charlie Chaplin and Gracie Fields both trod its boards in the early days of their careers.

The first playhouse on the site was opened in 1865. The foundation stone was laid by builder G.B. Scotson's four-year-old daughter who was presented with a suitably inscribed silver trowel for her troubles. The ceremony on October 26, 1864 was followed by a celebration meal in a Northgate restaurant run by a Mr G. Laws where speeches about the educational and amusement value of drama were duly applauded. It took the name of the Theatre Royal, although it was anything but regal inside. The ceiling was unplastered and the poor class of patrons it attracted had to sit on uncomfortable wooden benches. Manager James MacDonald once got so fed up with the unruly commotion in the crowd when he was playing Rob Roy, he jumped off the stage in his kilt, threw the troublemakers from the gallery out on to the street and then climbed back under the spotlights to resume the drama. During another play an imperious Arab chieftain demanded: 'Bring forth the fiery, untamed steed of the desert!' An ancient white horse belonging to a local dealer hobbled on stage and the audience instantly recognised it and collapsed into hysterical laughter.

But promoters found great difficulty in making drama pay. On December 2, 1868, the Northgate door receipts totalled just seven shillings so the manager refused to allow the show to go on. The Theatre Royal closed and was pulled down in 1873.

A new theatre sprung up in its place in 1881. It was opened on September 26 and was widely regarded as 'the prettiest little theatre in the North of England, having a classic facade of polished Dunhouse stone, decorated with masks of Shakespearean characters'.

For a couple of years it even managed to make a profit. But disaster struck on November 16, 1883. To mark a special benefit night for the leading lady Miss Rainbow, a fire-balloon was sent up before the performance of The Ticket of Leave Man. At the end a firework display was given. Next morning the theatre was found to be well ablaze, and, in spite of the efforts of the brigade, it was completely burnt out. All the costumes and personal affects of the actors went up in smoke but the town rallied round with a collection to make up for their loss.

The fire was believed to have started when a spark from the fireworks caught in the previous night's stagecloth which had not been put away properly. But theatre-types do not give up that easily. The Theatre Royal was rebuilt and reopened in 1887. This time it was heralded as one of the most up-to-date theatres in the provinces. It even featured tip-up chairs and the electric light made an impressive debut on stage. However, there must have been a lot of dramatic irony behind The Streets of Darlington production of June, 1891. The star performer was the municipal fire engine, complete with horses and firemen, which featured heavily in one of the scenes.

'NB: This is without exception the most realistic effect ever witnessed on any stage in England,' boasted the posters.

This time, though, they got away with playing with fire – unlike in 1883. For 49 years the theatre catered for the playgoing public of Darlington. It was often a struggle to make ends meet, and that struggle ended on October 10, 1936. The Charles Simon Repertory Players ended its 30-week run of a comedy called Bird In Hand and as the curtain came down for the last time the performers and audience joined hands to sing Auld Lang Syne. In 1949 the Darlington and Stockton Times remarked: 'There must be many play goers in the town who hanker after the atmosphere of the Theatre Royal with its old red plush, dirty gilt carving and scrollwork on the circle and boxes, and, of course, the orchestra playing an overture – an atmosphere that had instinctively put the audience into a recipient mood for a play by the time the curtain went up.'

It was a gamble that first brought actor Charles Simon, Radio's Dr Dale, to Darlington before the war. The year was 1936 and he was leading touring companies when a friend bet him £20 he could not make a hit in the town. He won the bet, stayed in the town and the Darlington Repertory Theatre was born. After that final performance, the Theatre Royal was demolished and a super cinema owned by Associated British Cinemas was built on the site at a cost of £50,000. It was opened by the town's Mayor, Coun J.H. Taylor, on January 31, 1938. The only link between the old playhouse and the new filmhouse was the adoption of the name Regal – a synonym for Royal – but that too has gone now.

But by the time the curtain came down at the Theatre Royal for the last time Darlington's other theatre, The Hippodrome

Charles Simon – brought rep to the town

17

and Palace of Varieties, had been going for more than 30 years. In 1904, with a town population of 50,000 and the Theatre Royal in Northgate holding a capacity of 1,000, the Darlington Hippodrome Company took the ambitious step of buying from the council a piece of land next to St. Hilda's Church. The existing buildings were demolished and the corporation started widening the road. From Italy came Rino Pepi, a showbiz figure of some note, and he leased the New Hippodrome and Palace of Varieties from the company and took over as manager. He struggled, but the theatre had taken a special place in the hearts of the townspeople. The only train into Bank Top station on a Sunday was dubbed the 'fish and actors' as it carried the chip pies' fish supplies from Grimsby and the following week's supply of variety performers.

In 1924 the Hippodrome was sold to a Newcastle businessman. Seven years later in August the first talkie graced the screen and the theatre recovered sufficiently for the BBC to do occasional broadcasts from the stage. The closure that had been on the cards for so long came in 1933 but by October Edward J. Hinge had come forward and reopened the Hippodrome with plans for a part-time theatre with one week being devoted to films, the next week to variety. After a 20-year struggle Mr Hinge gave up and the curtains came down on June 16, 1956 – ironically on a production called Happy Go Lucky.

The Darlington and Stockton Times wrote: 'Two generations have grown up with the Hippodrome and have talked or will talk of gay nights there with the same sense of regret for vanishing youth and departed pleasures as Shallow recalled having heard the chimes at midnight. And now it must close because the public no longer wants what it has to offer.'

But within two years the Hippodrome was back in business. The Darlington Operatic Company had found itself homeless when the Hippodrome shut so in August 1958 it formed a non-profit-making organisation called the Darlington Civic Company. The council pitched in with a grant of more than £1,000 and the theatre reopened. There followed six financially perilous years. In 1961 the theatre was up for sale but the operatic company successfully renegotiated its lease. Eventually on November 10, 1964, the council bought the theatre for £8,000, despite it needing an estimated £6,000 for refurbishment. Over the next few years the seating was reduced to 601.

The update was finally finished in accidental fashion when an ICI tanker turned into Borough Road bringing down the iron canopy with it. A new exterior added the icing to the cake. Theatre historians believe the ambitious appointment of Peter Tod, who at 24 was the

Handbills from the early days of theatre in Darlington

youngest director in the country, to the hot seat in January 1972 was important in establishing Darlington as a centre of cultural activity. The Civic – as it has been known since the Sixties – has gone from strength to strength. In 1982 the Friends of the Civic started raising £12,000 to replace every seat – a project that was completed in time for the autumn 1983 season to begin. In 1989 four houses in Borough Road were demolished so that a massive £1.5m expansion could begin, increasing seating capacity at the reopening in November 1990 to 915. The work included reopening the upper circle which had been closed for 30 years. Further confirmation of The Civic's importance came in the summer of 1991 when the Royal Shakespeare Company announced it would play there. The RSC was so impressed by the updated Civic it decided to add Darlington to its list of 16 venues in this country and four in Europe.

BERNHARDT
GALLERY

Come and see a wide range of original Watercolours and Etchings

Many reasonably priced Limited Edition Prints

Piers Browne new book on Wordsworth available in Gallery

Now showing Judith Bromleys outstanding pastels of the Dales

**60 CONISCLIFFE ROAD,
DARLINGTON
Telephone. 356633**

SWALLOW KING'S HEAD HOTEL

As well as our Northgate Restaurant, and excellent reputation for funtions of all kinds from
APRIL, 1992
we offer new accommodation in our Cornmill Wing.
A brand new Reception and improved facilities.
In fact everything you could want from a hotel; situated conveniently in the centre of town

The Beeswing Inn

East Cowton (Northallerton)
Want to get away from it all?

Come and relax in our cosy Lounge and soak up the atmosphere by our open coal fires. With an extensive range of home-made foods and a tantalizing wine menu, speciality sweets, prepared with the extravagant in mind.

★ Bedrooms with en-suite facilities, colour TV
★ Bar Lunches 12 noon-2 p.m. Tuesday-Saturday
★ Traditional Sunday Lunch 12 noon-1.30 p.m.
★ Evening meals 7 p.m.-10 p.m.
Bookings welcome
Telephone: (0325) 378349

Visa/Access welcome

33 GRANGE ROAD
DARLINGTON
(0325) 467570

FLORAL DESIGNERS   BRIDAL STUDIO

A Fabulous Range of Designs

Including Caroline, Alexander, Lynn Lundie, Fiorito, Beverly Summers, Anna Christina, Lynn Ashworth

SHOES by Meadow, Anello and Davide

HEADWEAR by Silk and Florentina, Jayne Bridal including our exciting new range of co-ordinating Headdresses and Bouquets
Also an Aladdin's Cave for the Flower Arranging enthusiast

Appointments preferred, but callers welcome

Tricia's Smart Set

Ladies Fashions
Dresses ★ Skirts & Blouses for every occasion

Personal service in friendly atmosphere
Our customers are left to browse at their leisure

Open 10.00 am to 5.00 pm excluding Wednesday

85 Parkgate Chambers,
Borough Road, Darlington
Telephone (0325) 283677

21

UNVEILED TODAY

ST JOHN'S MOTORS
INVITE YOU TO THE LAUNCH
OF OUR FLAGSHIP EXECUTIVE SALOON....

The new Toyota Camry.

Camry V6 GX
£22,325†

**"Only when the
body is truly relaxed
can inner peace
be attained."**

The new Toyota Camry
represents a quiet revolution.

Whilst total quality has been
designed in, virtually all noise has
been designed out.

And, in terms of technology,
comfort and looks, the Camry is a
class-beater, even by luxury
executive saloon standards.

Its all alloy, 3 litre 24 valve V6
engine will whisk you from 0 to
60 in under 9 seconds. As for
creature comforts, the V6 GX

gives you a 6-speaker RDS stereo
system, leather upholstery, electric sunroof, electric windows,
ABS braking, air conditioning and
a catalytic converter.

Like all new Toyotas, the
Camry comes complete with a
free 3-year/60,000 mile warranty,

6-year anti-corrosion warranty
and a year's free RAC member-
ship.* The Camry range starts at
£17,520.†

To test drive the car that's on
everybody's lips, pay us a visit.
We think you'll be quietly impressed.

*See us for full details.

†Price includes car tax and VAT but excludes delivery charges of £298 (incl.
VAT), number plates and road fund licence.

Prices correct at time of going to press

**ST JOHN'S MOTORS
(DARLINGTON) LTD.,
NEASHAM ROAD,
DARLINGTON.
TEL: (0325) 482141
ASK FOR IAN, SIMON OR NEIL**

🚗 **TOYOTA CAMRY**

H. TAYLOR & SONS

The Noted PIE SHOP

(Established 1924)

Best Quality Beef, Pork and Lamb

A variety of Pies, Sausage, Cooked Meats, Pate and Cheese

FREEZER MEAT UP TO 12% DISCOUNT

Fresh Farm Turkeys and Chickens for your Christmas Dinner

Also Best Quality Show Beef

★ **ORDER EARLY FOR CHRISTMAS** ★

41-45 Skinnergate, Darlington

Tel. Darlington 464716

NORTH ROAD STATION

- Step into the past at our restored Victorian station building on the original route of the Stockton & Darlington Railway

- See Stephenson's LOCOMOTION and many other exhibits relating to the railways of North East England

For opening times, prices and further information

Tel: Darlington (0325) 460532

A leisure facility of Darlington Borough Council

AFTTI   44-073

T.V.
——— VIDEO

WHERE can you

RENT OR BUY

The latest Colour Television or Video Recorder at competitive prices and excellent After Sales Service?

Call — C. MIDCALF

108 Parkgate, Darlington.
Telephone 464636

WE Buy The Best —

Why Don't YOU?

k3376   AFSQW

23

FINE ART

TRADE GUILD

WILLIAM DODDS

(Established 1884)

Specialists in Picture Framing

Dealers in Fine Art, Oil and Watercolours, Signed Limited Editions, Sporting Engravings, Antiquarian Prints and Maps,

Sepia Photographs of old Darlington

Limited Editions by Gerald Coulson, Nigel hemmings, David Shepherd, Gordon King, Sturgeon, Antony Gibbs, Clare Eva Burton and many more well known artists.

Originals in Oils by David Morgan, Gordon Lindsay, Don Micklethwaite, Peter Greenhill, Christopher Osborne, Jean Hamilton George, Lesley Hammet.

Original Watercolours by Christopher Hughes, John Urwin, Peter Burke, Jack Green, Brian Steward, Janet Rogers

We also have **Dry point Etchings** by Henry Wilkinson and Peter Partington

34 TUBWELL ROW, DARLINGTON
Telephone 462599

DAVID WARD
ARCHITECTURAL AND SURVEYING SERVICES

A full range of surveying and design services are offered in the following fields

- *Site investigation, planning appraisal and development potential*
- *Detailed design work for all domestic, commercial and farmwork, including extensions, conversions and new build*
- *Full planning and building regulation applications, including consultation with Local Authorities*
- *Full preparation of plans, specifications, including contract management on all forms of development*
- *Preparation of reports on defects, dilapidations and schedules relating to all forms of property*
- *Structural surveys*
- *Preparation fo farm plans, acreage and all forms of cartography*
- *Advice on all forms of grants, including farm conservation and diversification. National Parks Barns Conservation Scheme, all grants from application, approval and claim*

Please contact D. Ward on Wensleydale (0969) 22046

BJYQV   44-260

VG LATE SHOP
Hurworth Village, Darlington

★ Wines & Spirits ★
★ General Groceries ★
★ Butchery & Cold Meats ★
★ Fruit & Veg ★
★ Cigarettes ★
★ Confectionary ★ Videos ★

All at your local 8 till late shop!

Telephone (0325) 720249

A ncient art of long ago

R ose

O range

M arjoram

A ngelica

T hyme

H ealing herbs and flowers

E ach with it's own therapeutic value

R emoves stress from body and mind

A ssists healing with flowing massage

P romotes vitality

Y ou are restored to health and harmony

Sue Mellish S.P.Dip.A.
Member of the International Federation of Aromatherapists

Tel: 0748 850471

Set on the Banks of the River Tees in the village of Middleton-One-Row

THE DEVONPORT HOTEL

is ideally situated for your Wedding, Conference or Party

- ★ Sixteen comfortable en-suite bedrooms, all with television, radio and tea-making facilities are available for overnight accommodation
- ★ A choice of menu is offered from an extensive Dinner Menu in the Riverside Restaurant to more traditional Bar Meals in our Bistro
- ★ We also offer popular Sunday Lunchtime Carvery
- ★ Theakstons Ales are now available
- ★ Children are especially welcome

NOW UNDER NEW MANAGEMENT
WE ARE HERE TO MEET YOUR NEEDS

For a copy of either our Wedding, Christmas or New Year Party menus, please ring

Martin Langley on (0325) 332255

ATZGO   44-260

ALLIED ACCOUNTANTS

1st Floor,
2 Raby Street,
Darlington,
Co. Durham. DL3 7TE
Telephone
(0325) 465939

For all your accountancy requirements

BUNRB   44-260

Darlington Museum

Tubwell Row

FULL OF DARLINGTON MEMORIES

ADMISSION FREE

Copy service for old photographs of Darlington.

Souvenirs, Gifts and Local History Books

Mon., Tues., Wed., Fri. 10-1, 2-6
Thurs. 10-1 only, Sat. 10-1, 2-5.30

Tel. 0325 463795

A BOROUGH OF DARLINGTON LEISURE SERVICE

ANTIQUES

Victorian and Edwardian Furniture

BYGONES

ESTABLISHED ~ 1986

VISA

Fireplaces~Oak~Pine

BYGONES
3-5
McMullen
Road
DARLINGTON

(0325)
461399
380884

ESTABLISHED FOR OVER 30 YEARS

Panel Beating

Welding

Paint Refinishing

Insurance Company Approved

D. T. Mackenzie

 ACCIDENT REPAIR SPECIALISTS
the sign of QUALITY ASSURANCE

Haughton Road Garage
215 Haughton Road,
Darlington
Co. Durham. DL1 2LD
Telephone: Darlington 465045

BJTUG   44-260

CROMBIES
RESTAURANT - CAFE

Home-made Food at its Best
Without Doubt Worth a Visit

Quality Fresh Ground Coffee

Freshly Roasted Joints
Delicious Home Made Sweets

LUNCHTIME SPECIALS
SNACKS SERVED ALL DAY

Morning Coffee
9.00am-11.30 am
Lunchtime
11.00am-2.30pm
Afternoon Teas
4.00pm-6.30pm

FULLY LICENSED

**36-44 Tubwell Row,
Darlington. Tel. 464475**

k3403   AOELC

Grange Hotel

Beautiful Mansion.
Built approx. 1804 by J.
Backhouse
SOUTHEND,
DARLINGTON
Tel. (0325) 464555

★ Set in own grounds
★ Near town centre, rail and bus terminals
★ Within easy reach of Tees-side Airport
★ Rooms with private bath/shower and toilet
★ Radio, telephone and colour TV
★ Central heating
★ Facilities for interview/meetings and small functions
★ Ample car parking

Walworth Castle Hotel

Open all Day, Every Day to Residents and Non-Residents. Breakfasts, Morning Coffee, Bar Snacks, Afternoon Teas, Restaurant

**DARLINGTON, Co. DURHAM
Telephone (0325) 485470**

Choose from our delicious new a la carte, Table D'Hote or bar menus

LUNCHTIME CARVERY
Monday to Saturday, 12 noon till 2 p.m.
2 Carvery Lunches for just £5.95

TRADITIONAL SUNDAY LUNCH
**4-Course Silver Service £7.25
Carvery £4.75**

Don't forget our Sunday Night Quiz
In the Farmers Bar — fun for all!!

Anniversaries — Christenings
Wedding Receptions — Conference facilities

The most competitive rates in Co. Durham, in luxurious surroundings

Forthcoming Events:-
**Celebrity Dinners, Murder, Mystery Nights
Christmas Party Nights**

AHLLQ   Please ring for details   k3405

Rowland May LIMITED

SUPPLIERS OF ALL GOOD QUALITY
FLOOR COVERINGS AT
DISCOUNT PRICES!

● Carpets ● Vinyls ● Rugs ● Large stocks for immediate deliveries ● Free planning and quotation ● Suppliers of all ranges including: AXMINSTER, ADAMS, BMK, BRINTONS, CARPETS OF WORTH, COLOROLL, EGE, FIRTHS, GREENDALE, HEUGA, HUGH MACKAY, RYALUX, STODDARD, TINTAWN, ULSTER, WILTON ROYAL ● Chinese, Indian and Pakistani carpets and rugs ● Contract installations welcome and carried out by experienced craftsmen

Easy parking, find us just through Cockerton on A68 West Auckland Road

89-91 West Auckland Road, Darlington

DARLINGTON (0325) 467297

T·H·E
parkgate
press
L·I·M·I·T·E·D

COMMERCIAL PRINTERS & DESIGNERS

FULL COLOUR PRINTING · THERMOGRAPHERS

PRINT HOUSE · BOROUGH ROAD · DARLINGTON
CO. DURHAM DL1 1SW

TEL: (0325) 463207/463846

FAX: (0325) 483192

MURRAYS

Jack and Nora Murray with baby Frank and staff outside their first shop: 74 Durham Road (now North Road), Darlington in 1923

TIMES MAY CHANGE BUT NOT OUR QUALITY!

Traditional bakers and confectioners for 68 years where personal service still counts

Nine branches at your service

Cockerton ● Covered Market ● Haughton Green
Crown Street ● Morrison Centre in Darlington
ALSO
Richmond ● Northallerton ● And within Kwiksave,
Linthorpe Road, Middlesbrough ● Yarm

QUALITY BAKING AT ITS BEST

AJEFi   44-260

• SAVE £££'S • SAVE £££'S • SAVE £££'S • SAVE £££'S •

3-PIECE SUITES DIRECT FROM THE FACTORY AT PRICES THAT CANNOT BE BEATEN!

New 3-piece suites from only £199

KELSO Luxurious Suite with removable covers
Available in print and dralon
FROM ONLY £299

Attractive PINCH Quilted 3-piece suite
FROM ONLY £369

This is just a small example of unbelievable savings offered to you

FREE FREE FREE DELIVERY FREE FREE FREE

SOFA BEDS: Full metal action, available in cotton print or dralon from only £169

Plus many, many more suites to choose from at discount prices

ALL AVAILABLE IN A CHOICE OF COLOURS AT TRADE PRICES
We guarantee we will not be beaten for price, service or quality!

SEE FOR YOURSELF AT OUR MASSIVE DISCOUNT SHOWROOM

DISCOUNT SUITE CENTRE

King Street (near Hunt Salerooms), Darlington
Tel: (0325) 386777

OPENING HOURS:
AFUEE   9 a.m. - 5 p.m. Monday to Saturday   44-260

BORDGATE ROAD

WE ARE HERE

COMMERCIAL STREET KING STREET

COMMERCIAL STREET

• SAVE £££'S • SAVE £££'S • SAVE £££'S • SAVE £££'S •

30

The Silver Screen

Darlington in 1939 boasted more cinema seats per head of population than any other town in the country. The cinema names come from a past era of entertainment: The New Empire, Electric Picture Palace, The Court Kinema, The People's Palace, Scala and The Majestic to name just a few. In Darlington today there is just one.

The story of the cinema, a form of mass entertainment that provided a cheap night out for two generations of Englishmen and women, started with one of the great scientific innovations of the 19th Century: the cinematograph. The first commercial presentation of motion pictures was on April 14, 1894, in New York. Just over a year later the Lumiere brothers premiered the first public film show in Britain at the Polytechnic Institute, London, and in February 1896 a Herr Rosenberg announced 'the first appearance in Darlington of the latest wonderful invention, the cinematographer, living, moving pictures'. His show for three nights only was in the Central Hall. Admission was 6d, 1s and 2s, and pictures started rolling at 8pm with carriages for 10pm. The show included a ventriloquist, and the films were The Dentist's Chair, The Execution of Mary Queen of Scots plus footage of the Henley Regatta and Persimmon winning the Derby.

In the same year, Poole's Myorama put on shows in the Larchfield Street Drill Hall, but it was not until January 1897 that the movies really arrived when a large audience at the Mechanics Institute is reported to have been driven wild with excitement at the 'animated and life-like scenes'. Travelling cinemas used to come to Darlington in the early days twice a year for the May and November festivals. They used to set up underneath canvas in the Market Place and Lead Yard, and the show was always preceeded by an automatic organ blaring out the national anthem. Dancing girls and other variety turns were often put on outside the tents to attract customers.

In January 1901 the Edison Animated Photo Company hired the Central Hall for nine nights, and over the next few years the hall became the first permanent residence for the heroes of the silver

Above: The Gaumont Cinema, Northgate, 1964 ; Below: The Regal, Northgate, 1938

The Majestic in Bondgate pictured in the late 1940s

screen in Darlington. The film show took place on the same stage from which Benjamin Disraeli addressed the people of Darlington when he visited the horitcultural show in 1848. There were seats for 710 people, but the hall was not that luxurious and it became known as the Central Lopies. Because films were silent a pianist accompanied them or sometimes a man gave a running commentary over the top. Central Hall shows were known as Fenton's Pictures after the man in charge for 32 years, George Percy Fenton. The Central Hall became the Central Palace on August 22, 1910. Another picture pioneer in the town was James Joseph Wyne. In 1909 he opened the Picturedrome in Temperance Hall, Gladstone Street. He already had a long history in the new film industry as an agent but the Picturedome was his first venture into cinema. One of his first appointments was a 17-year-old usherette called Agnes. It is unrecorded if it was the back row of the Picturedrome on a Saturday night that sparked off their romance, but they later married and Agnes went on to become one of

The Empire Cinema at the junction of Quebec Street and East Street where the Presto supermarket is now. The picture was taken in October 1960 and the film showing was The League of Gentlemen starring Jack Hawkins and Richard Attenborough

the first women projectionists in the country. The Livingstone Hall in Northgate – so called because its opening in 1873 coincided with the death of Dr David Livingstone in Africa – changed its name to the Assembly Hall in 1910 and began showing movies.

In the same year Messrs Clarke and Moscrop were commissioned to design the first purpose built cinema for Darlington. They were probably given instructions not to emulate the first ever cinema in Britain which opened in Picadilly Circus, London, on March 21, 1896, and was gutted by fire two weeks later. On June 23 1911 – the day after the coronation of George V – the New Empire Electric Picture Palace opened on the corner of East Street and Quebec Street where Presto's town centre supermarket is today. Naturally enough the first pictures were of the previous day's coronation. Due to the Empire's spacious lounge it was christened The Hall of 1,000 Lights. It took 900 people, and admission was 2d, 3d, 4d, 6d, and 1s. Local artists were engaged to sing well-known songs which were illustrated by coloured pictures on the white wall screen.

As Agnes and James Wyne discovered, cinemas were an ideal place to start romances and the Empire positively encouraged naive skullduggery among patrons. Every night when the doors opened there would be a rush to get the seven double seats on the back row that were built to take two in comfort. When the Empire opened, the Wynes transferred their skills from the Picturedrome which shut in 1913. On one celebrated occasion, James placed one of his more portable projectors in a handcart and wheeled it up to Polam Hall School where he put on an educational film for the pupils. Because of the low social standing of the cinema the girls were not allowed to go, so for many of them this was the first film of the lives. But the Empire was the start of a fashion that swept Darlington.

In August 1912, the Arcade Cinema opened in Skinnergate; on February 11, 1913, the Court Kinema just yards down the road opened; on March 17, 1913, the Scala Cinema in Eldon Street showed its first film followed by the Alhambra in Northgate just five days later. On the opening of the Court Kinema in Skinnergate The Northern Echo wrote: 'We may even go beyond the modern era to the time when Rome was at the height of prosperity when thousands flocked to the stadiums to see gladiators wield their weapons in the fierce bullfights and say that even that did not have the allurements and fascination so characteristic of the modern kinema shows.' The town seems to have gone cinema mad. When the Court Kinema was opened The Arcade cinema only yards away was so popular a second gallery was already being built. The Arcade had 800 seats, 450 of them priced at 3d, and the more expensive 6d and 1s seats had the luxury of their own exits onto Bondgate. The cinema management boasted that all the candelabras in the main hall had 2,000 candlepower bulbs. Because seats at the Arcade were relatively cheap, it attracted a plebian audience and specialised in Western thrillers. The Court Kinema, though, was a meeting place for the elite of the town. Its festooned oriel window is still above the Skinnergate arcade that bears its name. Like all the cinemas it specialised in films, but not exclusively. During interludes a darts player from Bishop Auckland would stand on the balcony and spit his arrows at a target on the stage 30ft away. He invariably hit the bullseye. The Arcade was steadily allowed to run down during the last few years of the Eighties. With the local government elections of May 1991, the Conservatives' plans to sell the arcade off to a developer who would build new shops were blocked. Instead the new Labour administration started looking for a housing association to turn what is left of the cinema into flats.

After the Arcade and the Court came the Scala. It was in Eldon Street and with a capacity of 1,000 was designed to cater for the growing north end of town. The Scala was also known as the People's Palace and the Essoldo. Just five days after the Scala opened on March 17, 1913, the Alhambra opened in Northgate on the site of Ivy House – a photographic studio. The Alhambra became known

THE NORTHERN ECHO, TUESDAY, 11 FEBRUARY, 1913.

The Court Kinema, Darlington.

The Last Word in Kinema Perfection.

Exterior of Kinema.

The opening of the Court Kinema reported in The Northern Echo in February, 1913

s the Gaumont and was considered the most luxurious of all the own's picture houses. The First World War put a halt to cinema building and the next major development was the arrival of the talkies. Once again, Central Hall was at the forefront, and in June 1927 George Fenton announced: 'You can now hear the pictures.' Two years later the Empire ventured into the world of sound installing talkie equipment at a cost of £6,000 and screening The Singing Fool starring Al Jolson. With four purpose built cinemas plus the New Hippodrome, the Theatre Royal and the Astoria – formerly the Assembly Hall, then the Ritz, then the Plaza before settling on the Astoria – all putting on films, one might have thought that even the voracious film-goers of Darlington might have been content. Not so. On Boxing Day 1932 the biggest and the best of the lot opened in Bondgate. It was called the Majestic and had cost £30,000 to build. As many as 1,600 patrons could be seated inside and its three-keyboard Compton electric organ made it a 'theatre-de-lux'. On that opening day 4,500 people crammed in to see three separate performances of the Maid of the Mountains. But Darlington was not finished yet. After years of dramatic struggle the Theatre Royal opposite Corporation Road in Northgate was pulled down and replaced by the Royal Cinema – later renamed the Regal and now the Cannon. The town's last cinema opened in June 1939. It was the Regent in Cobden Street built by Thompson's of Middlesbrough to hold 1,050 people in the growing Eastbourne area of town. The first film screened there was Angels With Dirty Faces starring James Cagney.

Darlington now boasted more cinema seats per head of population than any town in Britain. But developers were still not happy and planned another one. They drew up plans for the Ritz in 1936. It would have been on Abbotts Yard, Bondgate, but for some unrecorded reason the ideas never left the drawing board. But the developers were probably quite pleased they never got as far as putting the Ritz on the map, for as fast as they had been built, Darlington cinemas were converted or pulled down.

The first to go was the one that had started it all: Central Hall. In 1942 the Fentons sold out to Central Cinema Limited after 32 years of showing films there, but just four years later Central Cinema surrendered the remainder of its lease to Darlington Corporation for £1,050. After much alteration it became the Borough Treasurer's Office and now is part of the Dolphin Centre complex.

On August 15 1947 the Court Kinema in Skinnergate met its untimely end when a fire gutted it. The blaze did £60,000 worth of damage and killed Margaret Iceton, 76, who lived next door at 3,

Friend School Yard. She had been evacuated but returned to a downstairs room to retrieve a pair of shoes when the ceiling collapsed on top of her. The Court Arcade was built on the site 12 years later. In 1947 the Astoria also opted out of films and became the Royal Astoria Theatre. The auditorium was so large that lorries could drive underneath it to deliver scenery. The performing arts did not last long but the Astoria can claim to have produced some real stars. In 1945 the Charles Simons Repertory Theatre was forced out of the Gladstone Street Temperance Institute – formerly the Picturedrome – by a fire and after one night in the Mechanics Institute in Skinnergate and a couple of years at the Little Theatre in Kendrew Street Simons brought his actors to rest at the Astoria. The company leader went on to be a television star in The Bill, London's Burning and the Singing Dectective. Movies returned to the Astoria in 1952 for five years. In 1957 it became a restaurant, then a bingo hall before finally succumbing to developers in the early Seventies. The next to close after the Astoria was the Regent. Opened in 1939 in Cobden Street it was the shortest lived of all the purpose built cinemas. In 1959 it became a bingo hall and 30 years later it was turned into a nursing home.

And then there were four, but not for long. In 1960 the Empire, the first of them all, shut its doors for the last time. After much debate it was pulled down and now Presto in East Street stands on its spot. The Empire was soon followed by the Scala in Eldon Street. For three years before its closure in 1962, bingo sessions had pulled in extra custom between films, but with constant pressure from the punters for more housey housey the Weightman family – owners since it opened in 1913 – gave in. A bingo hall still thrives there today.

The Gaumont, originally the Alhambra, in Northgate was the fifth to close. The ring-road now runs past its door and Northgate House sits on its projection box. The Majestic in Bondgate fought a valiant rearguard action against closure. Opened in December 1932 it was renamed the Odeon in 1943 and had a facelift in 1968. With audiences flagging, organ recitals were re-introduced in 1974 in a bid to recapture some of the old atmosphere and two years later the modern idea of all-night films was tried.

But in 1978 it nearly went out with a very big bang when a burning Molotov cocktail was found under a seat. Eventually it went the way of all but one of the boom-time cinemas in Darlington, closing in 1981. It was reopened in 1986 as a snooker hall. Which left just one: The former Theatre Royal in Northgate. In 1977 ABC refurbished it putting in three screens and renaming it the Cannon.

Riverbank Tales

The parish of Darlington is watered by three rivers: The Tees, the Skerne and the Cockerbeck. It is from the banks of these rivers that many of the town's myths and legends have grown up. Perhaps the most immutable effect the waters have had on Darlington is that they caused it to have a name – although it is debatable which of the following derivations is the definitive one. In past centuries the town has been called Darningtun, Derlington, Deryngton, Darneton, Darrhton, Dearungtun, Dearningtun, Dernington, Dernigntune, Dearthington, Darnton and Dernton. 'Dare' meant water; 'ing' a meadow and 'ton' a settlement, which came together to form the town on the watery meadows – a reference to the time when the Skerne regularly flooded covering many acres. The Saxon word 'derne' or 'dearnenga' means secret, dark or hidden, or could refer to the sluggishness of the water. At one stage it seems likely that the Skerne was called the Dare and before that the Derne. Another theory suggests it was the Cockerbeck that was called the Dare and so the houses beside it became 'the town on the Dare's meadows'.

Alternatively one historian notes 'deor' or 'deorling dilectus' when allied with 'tun' for town or village would mean 'the chosen town built on holy land'. Another suggests the derivation is from 'the town of Deorn's son' as the Saxon word 'ing' meant son. Even more bizarre is the unfavoured suggestion that once upon a time there were only three farmhouses in the area. They were called Dar, Ling, Ton.

The Headless Hobgoblin of Neasham

Wherever the name came from it is indisputable that the town stands on these rivers and over the years the human population became convinced it was not alone in inhabiting the banks. Witness the remarkable tale of the Headless Hobgoblin of Neasham. 'Hob Hedeless' infested the road running from Hurworth to Neasham, but due to some strange physical deformity he was unable to cross the Kent – the small stream that runs into the River Tees at Neasham. Hob was a kelpie, an evil spirit, who sat by the side of the Tees and lured women and children and easily-led men to him. He then took them into his subaqueous abode where – and history contradicts itself at this point – he either ate them whole or caused the river to swell way above its usual levels so they drowned. Naturally the Headless Hobgoblin of Neasham was public enemy number one, particularly after he was heavily implicated in the death of Robert Luck, a Darlington brick-layer. Tragic Robert was said to have come across old Hob on the Hur-worth to Neasham road and sadly perished in the murky depths of the water on December 31, 1722. So the brave villagers grouped together and had the impudent Hob exorcised and he was laid under a large stone for 99 years and one day. If anyone sat on the roadside stone they would be glued there forever. Whether anyone ever got in a fix on the stone is not recorded, but when the road was rebuilt around the turn of the 1800s the resting place of the Headless Hobgoblin of Neasham was fearlessly removed and he was never more seen again.

Peg-Powler of The Tees

In place of the hobgoblin came the dreaded Peg-Powler of the Tees who, with her horrible green hair, was an awful sight. Parents would warn their children 'Peg-Powler will get you' if they ventured alone on the riverbank. Apparently, 'Peg-Powler with her green hair' would jump out, snatch the infant and drag it into her watery chambers. Peg-Powler seems to have been a 17th Century invention to keep kid-dies away from a dangerous playground and in the eighteenth century she became surplanted by the Boggly-Bo that also had a unusual pen-chant for drowning people. For some strange reason defying old Bog-gly-Bo became a test of manhood and so is believed to be one of the derivations of the phrase 'saying boo to a goose'. But towards the end of the last century Peg-Powler was reincarnated as a male and made a come-back, cleaning up his new-found male image in the process. Indeed, a rumour circulating in Middleton St George in the Twenties was that he had dragged a drowning lad from Tommy's Hole, a swirlpool near Middleton One Row, and saved his life.

And, centuries earlier the people of Darlington had cause to thank a kindly relation of Peg-Powler, Boggly-Bo and the Headless Hobgoblin of Neasham. Hob the benevolent sprite was said to hang out in caves in Runswick Bay, Hartlepool and Sunderland and was so well-known for its healing properties people would take their children suffering from whooping cough there. Carrying the sickly babe, the parent would enter the cave and summon up the sprite thus:

'Hob-hole Hob!
My bairn's getten t' kink-cough,
Tak't off, tak't off!'

The Great Flood

If the odd inhabitants of the riverbanks were not inticing people to watery graves the rivers themselves would give it a try. Both the Skerne and the Tees used to have a serious propensity towards severe flooding. In February 1753, the Tees rose 15ft above the high water mark and demolished the turnpike house at Croft, taking £50 of the road money with it. A little further downstream, the tidal wave engulfed the village of Neasham. In March a Mr Johnson wrote in a letter that: 'It drowned almost entirely all the village of Neesham, having destroyed every house except one, to which all the people resorted, and by good luck saved their lives, though with the loss of all their cattle and stacks of hay and corn'.

One morning in November 1771 Mr Hill of Blackwell got out of bed, pulled back his curtains, and discovered an odd assortment of coffins lying in his garden. They had been washed there by the swollen River Tees and, although Mr Hill probably did not know it at the time, he was in the middle of what Darlingtonians came to know as 'The Great Flood'. The coffins, complete with bodies, had been swept several miles downstream from Gainford where seven yards of the church-yard were taken away by the current.

Croft was again badly waterlogged, with the church flooded out and the church gates carried away. It is said the house of an elderly couple in the village was so submerged that they abandoned it completely and took to the roof. For hours they clung to an overhanging tree watching the water washing in and out of their bedroom window. Eventually the old woman could keep herself up there no longer. She let go of the branch and fell through the roof into the murky waters flushing around her house.

In a truly touching moment of devotion the husband cried: 'No, my dear, as we have lived 40 years happily together, so let us die in peace and love.' He too relinquished his grasp on the branch and tumbled through the roof towards his end. But the water had subsided and the upper floor of the house was damp but strong enough to support both of them. And they lived happily ever after – although probably not long enough to witness the swelling of the Skerne in 1875. 'At about one o'clock wakeful ears heard the lippering of water on doorsteps. A few watchful eyes saw the danger of a serious flood. Many, however, slept soundly on and awoke to find deep, yellow muddy water in the lower rooms of their houses,' The Northern Echo recorded on October 22. Heavy rain was responsible and people living in the Clay Row area of town suffered most. In their houses water 3ft deep swilled around. At the gasworks in John Street the water reached 6ft deep turning quickly to steam when it hit the white-hot generators causing the town's lights to go out. In the cellar at the Lord Nelson Inn, Parkgate, The Northern Echo reported that barrels of beer and spirits were 'swimming about'. 'It is feared that some of the contents may be reduced below proof but up to last night this had not been ascertained,' wrote the journalist, getting his priorities right. But the only casualties of the deluge were two pigs and a pet fox, although one 'well-known Darlington character' had a close shave in Park Street. The newspaper speculated as to why the character was 'more than ordinarily somnolent' and hinted that his famed appreciation of liquor may have been the cause. 'At any rate, he was oblivious of the flood until finding one side cold he put down his hand and discovered it was wet. He turned over in astonishment when lo and behold! the other side shared a similar fate.

Leaping out of bed the unlucky fellow plunged bodily into the flood and, as he phrased it, became 'all o'er wet'. Outside in the street, old codgers were agreeing this was the worst flood in living memory. Entrepreneurs were out making money. Cart-owners were charging 1d or 2d for a lift and strong men were piggy-backing people across the floods. This financial venture was successful until one man collapsed, throwing his passenger headfirst into the water. Just as soon as the floods had subsided they were back again. The rains came on November 14 and the river broke its banks on November 15. The Northern Echo said: 'From the point where the road rises to Haughton to where it rises to Victoria Road, Darlington, was a miniature plebeian Venice.'

Refugees were taken to the Central Hall where soup kitchens were set up. This time there were even fewer fatalities – just one pig belonging to the chimney sweep. Butcher Mr Trees made sure his prize porker got away safely by sitting it in a specially-built chariot and towing it through the floods. A doctor visiting the sodden area of town was seen lying in a cab with his head out of one window, his feet sticking out of the other. The cushions were floating in the water which was about 6ft deep, but he was dry. About 800 houses and 3,000 people were affected.

Murder on the bank

Aside from floods and fatal meetings with evil sprites, the other lethal aspect of the riverbanks was that they were the Darlingtonian's favourite place to murder his enemy. Late on the night of Saturday June 6, 1624, Xpofer (Christopher) Simson of Thornaby, who was travelling to Aldborough, was found strangled with weavers' twine on Baydale Banks between Darlington and Low Coniscliffe. The coroner held an inquest on the Sunday morning. Ralph Simpson of Aldborough was arrested, tried, convicted and was languishing in Durham Gaol by midday. Ralph, a weaver, was found to be carrying bloodied twine and certain items of the dead man's property. He claimed to have been in Low Coniscliffe on the fateful night because he wanted to get to Darlington early on Sunday morning to buy a new pair of boots – a claim that did not hold water in the eyes of the jury.

The 14-man jury placed the circle of bloodied twine found in Ralph's possession around the dead man's neck, and found it fitted perfectly. Their judicial report continues: 'And wee caused the said Ralph to handle the bodye; and upon his handlinge and movinge, the body did bleed both at mouth, nose and eares.' Evidence enough. Ralph was convicted of murder 'by the instigation of the Devell or of somme secret malice' and driven immediately to Durham Gaol. Many a ballad was written on the subject, but only one verse from The Baydayle Banckes Tragedy still remains:

> O Blackwell is a lovesome vill! and Baydayle Bankes are bright!
> The Sabbath breeze the crystal Tees with wavelets has bedight;
> Its oaks and elms are cool and thick, its meadows should be green,
> But there are blades of deeper shades, a bloody red is seen.
> Come tell me, child, my Averil mild, why harried thus you be?' –
> Father! there is a murthered man beneath yon greenwood tree.' –
> Ho! neighbours mine, – here Cornforth bold, and Middleton of might,
> For there hath been a slaughter foul, at Baydayle Head last night'.

Another celebrated murder occured on Sunday January 5, 1840. John Chisman of Blackwell Mill and Mr Rutter were strolling along the bank of the River Skerne about three hundred yards from the mill when they spotted what looked like 'a flannel petticoat'. Curiosity getting the better of them on a lazy Sunday afternoon, they wandered off to a nearby farm and collected a hay-fork. After poking around on the river bank they skewered the surprise of their lives: a female body. They dragged it out and carried it to the granary at the mill where the following day William Trotter, Darlington coroner, held an inquest. The evidence showed that the deceased was a young Coventry woman, Susan Dagley, who had been working at Pease's Mill for nine months. About five weeks earlier she had gone missing from her lodgings in Priestgate. According to Victorian pathologist Arthur Strother who examined the body, the arms and hips were badly bruised, the lungs healthy, the brain much gorged with blood and there was no appearance of pregnancy. His opinion was Susan had been murdered and her body thrown into the river. Another Priestgate lodger, Thomas Brownrigg, was immediately arrested. A hastily convened court heard that on Friday November 29, 1839, Susan had stormed into her lodgings at about 7.30pm, thrown her tea-tin on the table, and stormed out again without saying a word. Brownrigg had left the house at 7pm and when he returned at 9.30pm he asked a third lodger, Woodhams, if he had seen anything of Susan. Without waiting for a reply he asked the old landlady, Jane Scott, the same question.

The court was told that four days later Margery Newton had seen Brownrigg coming up from the water in a stooping position at 7am. On this evidence alone Brownrigg was convicted of 'wilful murder against some person or persons unknown'. His sentence is unrecorded although it is unlikely that it had any connection with the waters of the town's rivers.

Ducking stool

In Roman times, there was little as exhilarating as seeing a good Christian being punished for his faith as he was tossed to the lions. In Darlington there was a similar hazy line between public entertainment and judicial punishment, and perhaps the most popular form of chastisement was the ducking stool. Only women could be admonished in this way. If they were found guilty of flagrant nagging or being addicted to bickering – there is an apparently medical term, communis objurgatrix, for this condition – they would be taken to the ducking pond near the River Skerne off Northgate. There they were tied to a cuckstool at the end of a long beam and immersed in the water until they stopped babbling. Darlington courts were particularly fond of this punishment at the start of the seventeenth century. In 1614, Jane Wilson and Rose Little were found 'guiltie of an unseemelie assault and an open scoldinge betwixt them in the open marquet' and were summarily ducked three times each. A common scold like Dorothy Metcalfe, who was a scourge on her husband George and a frightful nuisance to her neighbours, was sentenced in 1618 to be 'furthwith sett on the Cuckstoole and ducked according to the custom of the Borrowghe'.

In 1620 the wife of Henry Beecrofte – she was not even considered worthy of having her own name recorded for posterity – was drenched for being a disgraceful 'evisdropper'. There is a suggestion that the Cocker Beck, which runs close to where the Northgate ducking pond was, got its name from this commendable practice – it is the 'cuck-her-beck'. However entertaining a spectacle, there is evidence to suggest that it was not the most effective of sentences. Four years after being well and truly ducked, that well-known affliction on silence Dorothy Metcalfe was back before the court for 'again being a common scold, and making a savage attack on an afferror in the performance of his duty'. She was fined heavily the second time around.

Hell's Kettles

Usually the townspeople of Darlington have held their rivers in great esteem. The Tees, which even merits a mention in Edmund Spenser's poem Marriage of the Thames and Medway, was loved for its eccentric curves and brilliant salmon. The sluggish Skerne – or Skyren – was applauded for the industry it could support. In 1810 along 13 miles of its banks through Darlington there were 12 mills: seven corn, two spinning linen, one wool, one fulling mill and one for grinding glasses. But sadly there was one particular stretch of water for which no-one had any affection.

> *And the nymph of the River Tees spake thus:*
> *'Then do I bid adieu*
> *To Befnard's battled towers, and seriously pursue*
> *My course to Neptune's Court; but as I forthright run,*
> *The Skerne, a dainty nymph, saluting Darlington,*
> *Comes in to give me aid; and being proud and rank,*
> *She chanced to look aside, and spyeth, near her bank,*
> *Three black and horrid pits, which for their boiling heat*
> *(That from their loathsome brims do breathe a sulphurous sweat)*
> *Hell's Kettles rightly called, that with the very sight,*
> *This water nymph, my Skerne, is put in such affright,*
> *That with unusual speed she on her course doth haste,*
> *And rashly runs herself into my widened waste.*

Hell's Kettles pictured in 1957

Truthfully, these are the words of Michael Drayton, a poet from the reign of James I who embarked upon a mammoth project: writing the history of England in poetic verse. He was so struck with the Tees that the nymph entered his soul and he poured out her thoughts. The Tees' hatred of Hell's Kettles was an emotion commonly felt in the area. They were a sinister place where ducks disappeared and Godless farmers spun through eternity. Sadly none of it is true – the two remaining pools are fed by a spring and were caused by subsidence in 1179 – but the myths are well-worth repeating.

In the beginning there were three boiling, bottomless pools – the smallest was filled in by Durham County Council in the Fifties when widening the A167 – formed by a horrific earthquake. 'In the land of Lord Hughe, the Bishop of Durham, the ground rose up to such a height that it was equal to the tops of the highest hills and higher than the towers and spires of the churches and so remained at that height from nine in the morning till sunset.

'But at setting sun, the earth fell in with a horrid crash and all who saw that strange mound and heard it fall were so amazed that for very fear many died, for the earth swallowed up that mound and where it stood was a deep pool.'

This was written by the Abbot of Jervaulx, a chronicler, reporting on the tumultuous events of 1179, and from that day on the rumours abounded. First there was the strange case of the duck, which one of

46

Henry VIII's inspectors painted with the mark of the Bishop of Durham and put it on the pools. It turned up a couple of days later in the Tees at Croft and so proved incontrovertibly there was a subterranean passage connecting the kettles and the river. This was confirmed by the 'man of colour', a diver from the Far East who took his life in his hands and threw himself into Satan's pits. He ended up in the River Skerne, having been sent along the underground channel. And then there was the bizarre tale of the irreligious farmer who could not get out. He insisted on working on St. Barnaby's Day saying: 'I'll hae my cart load of hay whether God will or nay'.

No sooner had the words left his lips than he was swallowed up by Hell's Kettles, and locals said on a clear day he could be seen drifting many fathoms deep doing eternal penance. Daniel Defoe was not impressed. The author of Robinson Crusoe took one look and dismissed the pools. 'Tis evident they are nothing but old coalpits filled in with water by the River Tees,' he stated. He was not quite right, but then neither were travellers' tales of the pools boiling. But the myths continued into this century. Ancient records claim the largest pike caught in England was found at Hell's Kettles, and in 1942 a fisherman reckonned he caught a pike nearly five feet long and covered with short, spiky hair.

In 1958 killjoy divers exploded the myths. The pools were neither bottomless – 22ft deep maximum, they said – nor boiling – 42 degrees and cold, they said. In a world without fantasy it is best to try and think of Hell's Kettles, now a site of special scientific interest, as the creation of the Devil during a bloody battle at the centre of the earth.

The Hell's Kettles Pike

A typical week in The Northern Echo

MONDAY

All the weekend's sporting action

TUESDAY

ECHOES

A magazine for grown-ups

WEDNESDAY

Eating Owt

- *Award-winning writer Mike Amos takes an offbeat look at the region's culinary delights*

THURSDAY

Pages of situation vacant adverts

FRIDAY

7 PLUS DAYS

All the week's TV plus what's on in the region

SATURDAY

PROPERTY*Echo*

Your guide to the best of the property market

■ THE NORTHERN ■

ECHO

You can't afford to miss it

The Northern Echo

PHOTO~SALES

The Northern Echo

QUALITY COLOUR AND ATMOSPHERIC BLACK & WHITE PRINTS FROM £4.00

Have you seen a special picture in **The Northern Echo?** Copies are available for you to purchase as a keepsake, or perhaps as a gift for a relative or friend.

In order to gain the best possible atmospheric effect, some photographs have been captured in black and white only, so please bear this in mind when placing your order(s).

Photographs are available in 8" x 6" at £4 each and 12" x 8" at £5 each (the cost includes postage, packing and VAT).

To order your photograph(s), complete the panel below, and send it, together with a cheque/postal order payable to: **North of England Newspapers,** and a newspaper cutting of the photograph you require, to the address shown.

Name...NE

Address ....

....

Date Appeared	Page Number	Photo Caption	No 8" x 6"	Cost	No 12" x 8"	Cost	Total Payment

Send to: Photo Sale Department, The Northern Echo, Priestgate, Darlington, Co. Durham. DL1 1NF.

AWAVS

29-290

49

PLASTIC ROOFING

AT LOW LOW PRICES

TOP QUALITY

For Trade and DIY

TRIPLEWALL & TWINWALL

The ideal roofing for:

Conservatories ● **Extensions**
Carports ● **Greenhouses etc.**

TRIPLEWALL END VIEW

- 4mm, 6mm, 8mm, 10mm, 16mm thick
- Long life external coating
- Clear or bronze tinted
- Anti-condensation internal coating
- Lightweight, easy to cut and drill
- Full range of accessories
- Virtually unbreakable
- High insulation value
- Flame retardant
- 200 times stronger than glass

Ring for FREE samples, price list and information pack

THE CASH & CARRY GLASS COMPANY

Whinfield Drive, Newton Aycliffe
Telephone: (0325) 310520

Toughened single and double glazing at very, very competitive prices

DELIVERY ARRANGED THROUGHOUT THE NORTH EAST

BTYCD

44-073

50

GAZE
ELECTRONICS
(Established 1978)

O u r   e x p e r t
technicians can repair
any make of
★ Colour or Black
and White TV
★ Video Equipment
★ Radio Equipment
★ Car Radios
★ Microvawes
★ C a s s e t t e s

*Fast, efficient and Competitively
Priced*

Free local collection service. All work
with written guarantee

Tel Darlington (0325)
482344

132 Gladstone Street, Darlington

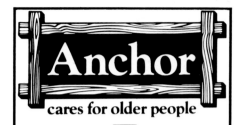

cares for older people

___

PATRON: HRH PRINCESS ALEXANDRA

ANCHOR IN DARLINGTON

Anchor is the major national provider of Housing and Care
Services for elderly people. We are a non-profit making
organisation. In Darlington we provide **sheltered housing**
to rent at:

* Greencroft Court, Greencroft Close
* Pembroke Court, Neasham Road
* Phoenix Court, Heron Drive

Sheltered housing to buy from Anchor's sister association
Guardian is available at:

* Guardian Court, Greencroft Close
* Witney Court, Greencroft Close

We also provide the highest standard of Housing-With-
Care for frail, elderly people at 'Elderwood',
Westmoreland Street in Darlington.

*For more information about our work and details of
accommodation please write to:*

**Anchor North, Park View House, Front Street
Long Benton, Newcastle-upon-Tyne**

Tel. (091) 270 2277

BKJKL   Charity No. 266004   44-260

POLAM HALL SCHOOL (founded 1848)

Independent Boarding & Day School for girls aged 3 - 18

★ Boarders from age 7
★ Excellent facilities for Science, C.D.T., Art & P.E.
★ Wide academic curriculum with 21 subjects available at Advanced Level
★ Comprehensive Careers Advisory Service
★ Strong tradition of Music and Drama
★ Extra-curricular activities include self defence, public speaking, golf and
   sailing
★ Duke of Edinburgh's Award Scheme
★ Scholarships are offered at 9+, 11+, 13+ and 16+
★ Government Assisted Places
   FREE education is available depending on income
★ Excellent road, rail and air links

A CARING EDUCATION FOR YOUR CHILD

For further information and a prospectus contact

The Headmistress, Polam Hall School,
Darlington DL1 5PA
(0325) 463383

AGGMC   45-260

51

A complete renovation service for all types of furniture

RE-UPHOLSTERY - Suites or odd chairs

RE-POLISHING - Suites to pianos

CABINET MAKING - All items repaired by expert craftsmen

A FREE estimate - only costs you a little time

ANTIQUES A SPECIALITY

Regency Furnishing

R. ROBINSON

29 Larchfield Street, Darlington
Telephone: 467091

ACOWC   49-260

ACTION ACOUSTICS

FOR SERIOUS HI-FI

A.K.G. Acoustic Research
Allison ● Audio-Innovations
Croft ● Cerwin-Vega ● Denon
J.B.L. Harman-Kardon ● Michell
Musical-Fidelity ● Philips

PINK TRIANGLE

Sennheiser ● Thorens ● Revolver
Revox ● Rogers ● Wharfedale etc

Sale and repairs

155-157 High Street, Redcar
(opposite Bus Station)

Telephone: 480723

AODUT   44-073

The Traditional Family Butcher
Established 19 years
Prime Cuts of Fresh Meat ★ Poultry & Game
Quality Cooked Meats
For personal attention visit

DAVID BECK, BUTCHER
Stall 34 Indoor Market, Tubwell Row,
Darlington. Tel. 0325 381091

ADTHF   44-260

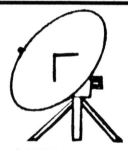

SATELLITE TV
VIDEO RECORDERS
COLOUR TELEVISION
AUDIO EQUIPMENT

Consult your local independent dealer

M. DENHAM
39 SKINNERGATE, DARLINGTON
or telephone (0325) 465384

LEARN TO
DRIVEWELL
WITH US

L.G.V.

L

P.C.V.

Modern Dual Controlled Cars
PSV and Heavy Goods Vehicles
Classroom Facilities
Manoeuvring Area

Drivewell Driving School
Darlington 468941

WHESSOE ROAD & (REGD OFFICE)
BOWMAN STREET DARLINGTON
Established 1962

Telephone
**(0642)
791235**

*Specialising in
Original Stripped Pine*

**Quality Victorian Furniture
restored to a high standard
and Hand-made
Reproduction Furniture
Furniture Stripping and
Polishing Service available
Pine Furniture made to order
Many beautiful items to
choose from**

*Why not pay us a visit today?
We are open 9-5.30
6 days a week*

The
Old Pine
Shop

**702 YARM ROAD
EAGLESCLIFFE
CLEVELAND TS16 0JE**

DARLINGTON ← A66 → STOCKTON

TEESSIDE AIRPORT
A67

WE ARE
HERE

YARM

AGHNH   44-260

Queens Head

*Main Road
Gainford*

Darlington
730958

**The charming village of Gainford with its pictureswque Village
Green adjacent to the River Tees, which offers excellent fishing, is
situated on the A67 Darlington to Barnard Castle road.**

The Queens Head is a village Public House
and Hotel.

We offer the benefit of two charming
restaurants: 'The Parlour' seating 35 and
'The Victoria Room' seating 65.

Our extensive menu is designed to meet all
tastes, with a selection of 22 starters and 36
m a i n   c o u r s e s .

Accommodation: All Bedrooms are with bath
ensuite, colour TV, tea making facilities and
central heating.

Telephone: (0325) 730958

Bishop Auckland GLAZING

1st for Choice
1st for Value
1st for Quality
1st for Service

New professionalk stained glass service using coloured glass church windows.

Huge selection of designs for doors, windows, screens, etc.

FOR THE VERY BEST IN WINDOWS AND DOORS

- uPVC
- HARDWOOD
- ALUMINUM
- PATIO DOORS
- BAY WINDOWS
- CONSERVATORIES

24 HOUR SERVICE

BISHOP AUCKLAND GLAZING

51, RAILWAY STREET, BISHOP AUCKLAND
TEL: (0388) 609942
FAX: (0388) 606387

54

SATELLITE TV
VIDEO RECORDERS
COLOUR TELEVISION
AUDIO EQUIPMENT

Consult your local independent dealer

M. DENHAM

39 SKINNERGATE, DARLINGTON
or telephone (0325) 465384

THE BUCK INN

Middleton Road, Sadberge
Darlington

Beautiful 17th Century Village Inn serving traditional beers and bar lunches 7 days a week.

Why not try our traditional Sunday Lunch £3.50 or children £2.50

Beer Garden and Play Area for the kids!

Telephone: 332416

BLJFC   50-070

MAKE A DATE IN YOUR DIARY!

HOLIDAY FAIR 92

Dolphin Centre, Darlington
Thursday, January 9, 10 a.m.-6 p.m.
Friday, January 10, 10 a.m.-8 p.m.
Saturday, January 11, 10 a.m.-5 p.m.
ADMISSION FREE

F-L-E-T-C-H-E-R
JOINERY

Traditionally the best Tradesmen not Salesmen

36 Haughton Green, Darlington. 0325 357347

| MR BURT IN THE OLD FORD 10 | GRANDAD'S OLD VAN |

Pages From the Scrapbook of a
Family Firm

"Burts carpets is as much a part of Darlington Memories as any local landmark. Almost every family in Darlington have bought carpet or floorcovering from Burts Carpets at some time. Burts have been selling carpets and providing an estimating, fitting and delivery service since 1945.

Long before 1945 though, the Burt family were trading in Darlington. A butchers and grocers, a local bus tour service, a taxi service, and even a coal delivery contract with Greenbank Maternity Hospital were all services provided by ancestors of the present company owners.

Burts Carpets has grown up too; from the small corner shop in Gladstone Street where it all started, and which still belongs to Burts. The company now has three larger stores, in Darlington, Stockton and Hartlepool, where you have a tremendous choice of stock rolls of carpets and floorcovering, rugs and famous name beds. There is also a smaller shop in Darlington where customers can browse and select from a full range of patterns.

So you see, it's not surprising that people keep coming back to Burts. We're delighted that you do, and we thank you all for your custom over the years. You could say, 'Hear next century's thrilling instalment' We hope your grandchildren will still keep coming to Burts Carpets for all their carpet and flooring needs!"

BURTS
CARPET WAREHOUSES

**Valley Street & Gladstone Street, Darlington. Tel. 0325 466470
Portrack Lane, Stockton. Tel. 0642 613577
259 Raby Road, Hartlepool. Tel. 0429 867099**

CONSERVATORIES

ADD DISTINCTION TO YOUR HOME

DESIGNED TO SUIT YOUR REQUIREMENTS

• • • •

Available in White and beautiful Woodgrained Mahogany finish uPVC.

AFVBB   K3386

NOW INTERNALLY BEADED FOR ADDED SECURITY

No High Pressure Salesmen

Just friendly advice to help you get what you 'WANT' at the 'RIGHT PRICE' with our personal service.

PHONE TODAY FOR OUR FULL COLOUR BROCHURE

BROCHURE HOTLINE

(0325) 300565

FOR MORE INFORMATION ON THE FULL RANGE OF WINDOWS, DOORS & CONSERVATORIES, COMPLETE AND RETURN THE COUPON TO:

KINGFISHER CONSERVATORIES

Freepost, Newton Aycliffe, Co. Durham. DH5 7BJ.

Name...

Address ....
....

You don't need the Radio Times or the TV Times...

...You only need The Northern Echo

7PLUSDAYS

7 Days Plus
FREE with The
Northern Echo
every Friday

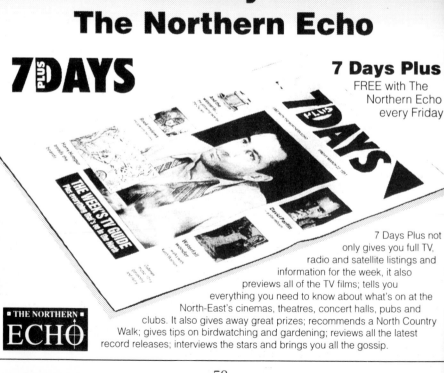

7 Days Plus not
only gives you full TV,
radio and satellite listings and
information for the week, it also
previews all of the TV films; tells you
everything you need to know about what's on at the
North-East's cinemas, theatres, concert halls, pubs and
clubs. It also gives away great prizes; recommends a North Country
Walk; gives tips on birdwatching and gardening; reviews all the latest
record releases; interviews the stars and brings you all the gossip.

THE NORTHERN ECHO

The Rogue MP

He was a Hungarian-Jew, a convicted thief and forger, a right-wing revolutionary who claimed to be a German spy, a Christian missionary, a womaniser and oil speculator who ended his life as a Buddhist monk in Tibet. His son was hanged for murder and yet he somehow managed to get himself elected MP for Darlington. He was the most notorious man ever to grace the town and quite probably the most preposterous conman in Britain in the 20th Century. For the year-and-a-half he touched base with Darlington he lived in Park View, Grange Road. He adorned every room with a picture of his hero Napoleon. The house was demolished in 1979 and replaced by a service station in a manner reminiscent of the way the town has tried to erase him from its collective memory. He was the only one of Darlington's MPs not to be afforded the common courtesy of 'esquire' in official records.

His name was Ignatius Timothy Trebitsch Lincoln, although by the end of his life the followers of his religious cult knew him as Abbot Chao Kung. His remarkable story starts on April 4 1879 at Paks on the bank of the Danube in Hungary. He was born Ignacz Trebitsch into a large family. One of his brothers went mad, another became a Communist revolutionary, a third was murdered by the Nazis and a fourth was arrested in America for sexual deviancy when trying to shop Ignacz to the police. During his early life in Budapest Ignacz rejected his father's Orthodox Jewish religion, tried twice to become an actor but failed and so instead became a journalist until police got wind of his habit of stealing gold watches. In 1897 he fled his home country, spent some time in Bristol and ended up in a Christian missionary's home in London where he stayed

Above: Trebitsch Lincoln's Darlington home, Park View in Grange Road.

until he stole his host's watch and returned ignominiously to Hungary. Back in Budapest he became editor of a spiritualist newspaper but in 1898 police received another complaint about a stolen gold watch. So Ignacz took off again.

This time he turned up in Hamburg where he met Margarethe Kahlor, the girl who was to become his wife. Although from a Lutheran family, she already had an illegitimate son, Julius Robut who later took the surname Tut. On Christmas Day, 1899, Trebitsch was baptised Ignatius Timotheus Trebitsch but he soon tired of Germany and sailed off to Canada where he exaggerated his way into a Presbyterian missionary. He stayed in Montreal until 1902, calling himself the Rev J.T. Trebitsch. He married Margarethe in July 1901. He managed to con the missionary organisation out of a fair amount of money, but resigned his post claiming they didn't pay him enough.

And so back to England in 1903 where he attempted to become an Anglican deacon but ingloriously failed his exams. He eventually latched onto Benjamin Seebohm Rowntree of York, a leading Quaker and Liberal, who used his family's confectionery profits to employ

Ignatius from 1906-1909. Ignatius travelled Europe taking his employer's name in vain on the pretence of researching a book that was to be the basis of the Liberal's social policy. He annoyed most British ambassadors on the continent by demanding access to sensitive information for his researches. The bulk of the book was written by August 1909, so Rowntree paid him off with a £10,000 loan – equivalent to about £500,000 today. The confectioner never saw the money again. By 1904 Ignatius had picked up the surname Lincoln – possibly out of deference to his other hero, Abraham Lincoln. And so Trebitsch Lincoln arrived in Darlington in early 1909. With the backing of The Northern Echo – then owned by Rowntree – he winkled his way into the local Liberal club. He was elected Liberal and Progressive Association parliamentary candidate on April 5, 1909 – even though he was not yet a British citizen. He told the party otherwise. Ignatius moved his family into Park View, and went off to Europe to pester more British officials. He returned to Darlington as the House of Lords rejected Lloyd-George's 1909 People's Budget, plunging the country into an unexpected General Election. Herbert Pease was Darlington's Conservative MP, first elected in 1898 to represent a seat formerly held by his father. Darlington had remained staunchly Tory during the Liberal landslide of 1906 due largely to the Pease family's influence. Before an election the girls in Pease's Mill would wear red knickers in honour of their man.

Trebitsch Lincoln had a mighty job on his hands, but he was backed all the way by The Northern Echo. The oratory skills learned when an unpopular missionary in Montreal were aired to devastating effect. Townspeople reported they were 'fizzled away' by his speaking. 'You are Britishers by the mere accident of birth. I am a Britisher by choice,' he told them. 'As politicians, men are absolutely and entirely useless and bankrupt.' The town agreed. Keen Liberals re-wrote the popular tune When Johnnie Comes Marching Home so the party faithful could sing it as they canvassed on Trebitsch Lincoln's behalf. Here are a few verses from a particularly attractive ditty called Parliamentary Election, January 1910:

When Lincoln gets to Parliament, Hurrah, hurrah,
And Pease is to retirement sent, Hurrah, hurrah.
No matter how the Lords may shout,
We mean to wipe their veto out,
For Lincoln leads us on to Victory.
'When Lincoln makes his maiden speech, Hurrah, hurrah,
For Right and Justice he will preach, Hurrah, hurrah,

For aged and infirm he'll crave,
T'extend the Pensions Liberals gave,
For Lincoln leads us on to Victory.

'When Darlington has spoken her mind, Hurrah, hurrah,
Lib'ral and Labour will be joined, Hurrah, hurrah,
We'll lead the Peers, oh! such a dance,
For meddling with Lloyd-George Finance,
They'll never touch the Budget any more.

'Lords, versus People, is the fight, Hurrah, hurrah,
So mind you do the thing that's right, Hurrah, hurrah,
Just put a X to Lincoln's name,
And get your mates to do the same,
For Lincoln leads us on to Victory'

Pease was labelled a food-taxer as he favoured import duties to protect British industries. He had also failed to vote in favour of old age pensions. Polling day was January 15, 1910. More than 95 per cent of the all-male electorate voted. Trebitsch Lincoln was confident. He

PROCLAMATION.

Be it known to you, O Men of the North, that the battle between the People and the Forces of Reaction starts at 8 o'clock this morning.

See to it that there are no laggards on the People's side.

Then **Victory** will be yours.

God Save the People!

stimated he would win with a majority of 30. Outside the Town Hall
rowds thronged in High Row, Blackwellgate and the Market Place
vaiting for the result. It was close. It went to a recount. At last, at
0.30pm, a message was projected onto a large screen: Lincoln 4,815;
'ease 4,786. A majority of 29 – chillingly close to Ignatius' prediction.
'he Conservatives were miffed and boycotted Rowntree products, but
'rebitsch Lincoln was on a roll. He took a party of workers to Bel-
;ium to see how poor life was under a protectionist government. On
eturn, he took them to Park View where he ostentatiously picked up
he phone, dialled a number and proceeded to sell hundreds of shares.
t was a spectatcular stunt – there was no-one at the other end of the
ine. But Mrs Lincoln became the first lady of Darlington, and when a
on was born on April 6, 1910 he was given Cuthbert as a middle
1ame for obvious reasons. Ignatius was not a great success in the
'ommons. One of his speeches displeased the Austrian government so
nuch it leaked out details of his past as a petty watch thief. MPs were
inpaid and Ignatius was a spendthrift and soon on the verge of bank-
uptcy, reduced to indiscriminate borrowing. Rumour and scandal
bounded and Trebitsch Lincoln had to go. The parliament elected in
anuary 1910 was the second shortest of the century and a week

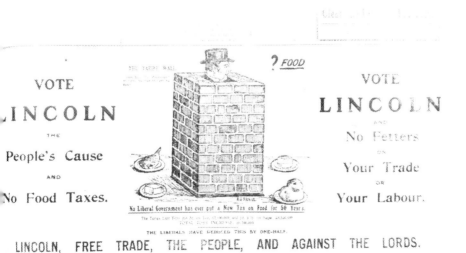

*On the vote trail. Left: An election day proclamation in The Northern Echo of
January 15, 1910. Above: Campaign literature labelling Pease a food-taxer*

before the December election the Rowntree family ensured Ignatius'
nomination was withdrawn. The Darlington Liberals were shattered
and sunk to defeat. Trebitsch Lincoln headed off into the sunset, vow-
ing to return. He never did. He headed straight for London and set up
two companies trading in Romanian oil. These promptly collapsed
ruining many shareholders and casting Trebitsch into even deeper
water. In a bid to keep himself afloat he turned to forging the signa-
ture of his former benefactor Seebohm Rowntree and others to secure
loans. The outbreak of The First World War in August 1914 saw
Trebitsch working as censor in Mount Pleasant Sorting Office. He
started writing on the letters he was supposed to be checking and so
had to resign. This left him with no income, no money and the loans
he had fraudulently taken out needing to be repaid. To add to his
woes a Romanian court sentenced him in his absence to seven months
jail for misappropriating money and goods from his oil companies. In
desperation, Trebitsch strolled to the War Office and tried to sell
them a cunning plan to destroy the German navy. They laughed him
out of the building so he went to Holland and tried to sell German
intelligence the same cunning plan. They were a little more impressed
by the former MP and tossed him a fragment of harmless information
to leak back to the British. Espionage proved not to be the lucrative
career he had hoped and so, with a net closing fast around him as
Rowntree had reported the fraud to the police, on January 30, 1915
at 5am Trebitsch left his wife and set sail for America on the liner
Philadelphia. On board he met and made love to a married woman
and her 26-year-old married daughter.

In New York he caught up with his brother Harry and accused him
of pilfering from him. Seeking revenge Harry tried to sell Trebitsch's
whereabouts to the police. They did not buy but instead had Harry
trailed. This led to his arrest and sentence to five years hard labour
for five offences of sodomy with another soldier. In May 1915
Trebitsch sold fantastically untrue stories of his espionage to the New
York World. The front page splashes made the British force the Amer-
icans to extradite him but his case was heard by German sympathiser
Judge Veeder. Scotland Yard sent over Chief Insp Ward to sort out
the procrastinating Veeder. The judge expressed surprise at Ward's
hurry and told him to tarry a while in America where at least he was
safe from the menace of Zeppelins. Ward returned home in a huff to
be killed by a bomb. It was dropped by a Zeppelin.

In custody Trebitsch bought time by pretending to help American
intelligence crack German codes. One day his warder took him for a
bite to eat and he escaped through a restaurant lavatory window

Lincoln and his party of workers setting off on their trip to Belgium

Eventually he appeared before a British court and on July 4, 1916, pleaded not guilty to forgery. The jury did not even bother to retire to consider their verdict and the judge sentenced the guilty man to three years in Parkhurst Prison.

On release in 1919 he was booted out of Britain and ended up in Germany as a right-wing revolutionary. With Col Max Bauer he masterminded the Kapp Putsch in 1920, a five-day rebellion which succeeded only in killing 3,000 people. In an outburst he said: 'The whole thing has crashed – these silly, thick-headed Germans.' But he immediately regrouped with Bauer and other disaffected characters in Hungary and formed the White International which planned to throw all Europe into revolutionary turmoil. A plot was hatched to murder Trebitsch, a Jew, who unsurprisingly fled, taking with him every White International document he could lay his hands on. He sold them to Czechoslovakian intelligence for £25,000 and they were published worldwide. Now apparently flush with money, Trebitsch summoned his wife from London. Then he discovered the Czechs had not paid him for his act of betrayal. In Vienna he sued them but wound up in prison for a week on a charge of entering Austria with false documents. Released on June 6, 1921, Trebitsch – by this time forbidden entry to practically every European country – announced: 'My desti-

nation is a profound secret. I shall disappear as if the earth had swal
lowed me and shall reappear in an unexpected quarter within eigh
years. Meanwhile, I shall accomplish my task.' He reappeared the fol
lowing year in darkest China as an ally of warlord Yang Sen – a leade
who threw his wife in a river in an attempt to emancipate women an
publically beat up his police chief for allowing pigs to roam th
streets. To improve Sino-European trade in 1923 Trebitsch took hi
Chinese pals to meet Bauer – the man he had betrayed – and a con
glomerate of dodgy businessmen. It was a successful mission and so
despite numerous sexual dalliances, he called his wife and two youn
sons to live with him in China. But Bauer and his partners droppe
out of the deal and Trebitsch had to flee an irate Yang Sen. Leavin
his sons on Java he and Margarethe sailed to Europe to gather mone
to buy an island plantation. In Germany Margarethe dumped him an
Trebitsch forgot about Java. The eldest son bravely earned enough t
send the youngest son to his mother, but then was caught by th
invading Japanese, brutally interned and finally committed suicide i
Australia. Trebitsch, exhibiting signs of madness, returned to Chin
where, on October 27, 1925, he saw the light in the Astor Hous
Hotel, Tientsin. In his biography he trumpeted: 'I made the grea
renunciation. I quitted the world. I forced the doors of the lunatic asy
lum open and walked out.'

He was converted at first to the Theosophist Movement, an 'eclecti
science of ancient and proved magic'. It was while staying in
Theosophistic monastery in Ceylon that Trebitsch heard his so
Ignatius had murdered a soldier at Trowbridge Barracks when drunk
Trebitsch rushed to Europe but failed to reach Ignatius before he wa
hanged on March 2, 1926. Not to be defeated he claimed to have com
municated with him through mysterious Buddhist telepathy.

From Holland he made his way back to Peking, calling himself
Ruh (meaning Rest) and Anagarika Pukkusati (The Homeless One
In May 1931 he was ordained a Buddhist monk and took the nam
Chao Kung prefixed by 'The Venerable'. He had 12 little stars o
nidanas branded into his scalp to symbolise the spokes of the Wheel o
Becoming. By June 1932 he had 13 disciples whom he took tourin
the world. Gradually they deserted him, especially when he was dis
covered in a compromising position with a young nun. In the lat
Thirties he was broke and demanding audiences with Roosevelt an
Hitler as an ambassador of world peace. Having lived out his las
years in Shanghai YMCA, our hero died on October 6, 1943, whil
undergoing an intestinal operation in Shanghai General Hospital.

St. Cuthbert's

even hundred years! The sun has risen and set, the trees have grown green and returned to golden, the bonny Tees congealed and thawed, but the church of God remained in all its beauty, like the pure expanse, to which its soaring spire directed the pilgrim's steps – seven hundred years, as near as may be. It is a long, long time. More than twenty generations have worshipped in their varying creeds and changing forms. Each of those races has passed into dust around it.

These poetic words were written at the end of the 19th Century and still the Lady of the North presides over the centre of Darlington, her spire standing 55 metres above the River Skerne. But when work started on her in 1180 there was no spire, just a tower rising no higher than the roofs on the transepts and naves. When the 150 ton spire was added to St Cuthbert's Church at the beginning of the 14th it caused the tower to sink about eight inches, and left much damage. Much of the church looks to be a little skew-whiff and some of the arches and pillars inside are no longer as round and straight as they were meant to be.

The settling required hasty shoring-up efforts which is why windows have been blocked up and an uneven supporting wall built under the tower. During repair work in 1899 medieval grave stones were discovered across the top of the tower. Much of this support work was undertaken between 1862-65. The foundations were primitive and widening cracks threatened the entire building. The building was reeking with damp and was rat-ridden. A further problem was the number of graves dug inside the church which removed some of the building's strength. When the floor was relaid it is said that three hundred skulls were taken from it in one day. Sir George Gilbert Scott was in charge of the restoration and one of his first jobs was to take down the boxes and pews suspended from the pillars. From 1700 galleries were put up throughout the church. Their floors were about 8ft above ground level and they were reached by wooden steps. In

67

1822 the church is thought to have seated 1,500 people. The maximum congregation now is about 400. These galleries and pews were rented or bought by the wealthy people of the town. Plans exist showing who owned which boxes upstairs suggesting the lower level was open to the plebians while those with money sat above. Surprisingly, the Quaker Pease family had a couple of boxes.

Bishop Le Puiset or Pudsey was the man responsible for St Cuthbert's. He chose a site where a Saxon church probably existed between 1003-16. The Saxon building does not seem to have existed at the time of the Norman Conquest. It is thought the church was not completed until about 1240. The choir stalls in the Chancel date from 1406. They were originally intended to seat the clergymen who were attending the college linked to the church. The hinged seats are properly called misericords – meaning mercy or pity – and there were originally 18. Only 11 remain because in 1838 a sub-curate decided to rip out a corner section, destroying three stalls. In its place he created a pew for Lord Darlington's family and knocked a hole in the wall so they could have their own private entrance. The stalls have since been replaced and the door blocked up.

At the east end of the Sanctuary is a mosaic reredos of the Last Supper by John Dobbin, perhaps Darlington's most famous artist. It is believed the work of art was intended for Westminster Abbey, but when the Londoners rejected it he presented it to Darlington.

The Curious Case of Cuthbert's Canonizing

The parish church of Darlington should really be called St Mullocke. For, according to one set of ancient historians, Cuthbert was originally christened Mullocke by Bishop Eugenie. Mullocke is Irish for Cuthbert and means 'illustrious of skill', and the infant in question was born in Ireland. Mullocke's mother was the daughter of King Murertack of Ireland, so he had royal lineage. Sadly, this ancient order of historians got their facts wrong. They made an easy mistake. Mullocke is much more likely to have grown up to become St Columba – which begins with a C but is one letter shorter than Cuthbert.

The real Cuthbert was born in Northumbria in about 637AD. When he reached the age of eight, he entered one of the most important years of his life. Both his parents died leaving him an orphan. Months later he was out playing with his friends when he tripped and damaged a knee. A three-year-old boy rushed up to him and told him to stop being so childish and dedicate himself to cultivating his mind. The youthful Cuthbert naturally declined, and the boy burst into

The Lady of the North and The Three Arch Bridge which was built in 1767

uncontrollable tears. Being a friendly sort, Cuthbert tried to console his young friend, who, through the sobs, told Cuthbert he was destined for great things. Cuthbert was converted, and an angel cured his swollen knee so he could walk properly. In the same year, his prayers are believed to have saved five ships in peril off the mouth of the River Tyne. He became a priest in his home town of Mailros and became well known for his miracles. Once when he was preaching, the devil set fire to a nearby house. Cuthbert saw through the evil spirit's trick, and the sham blaze disappeared. He is also believed responsible for extinguishing a conflagration at his nurse's house. She was the woman who looked after him following the death of his parents. One day she rushed up to him pleading for help as her home was burning. 'Fear nothing, for this fire will not hurt you,' he is reputed to have said. He lay on the ground in front of the house and prayed silently. 'Immediately a strong wind rose from the west and it turned the fire away without doing harm to anyone,' his biography records. He joined the monastery on Lindisfarne for 12 years, but the lifestyle there proved too hectic for his liking so he retreated to a single cell on Farne Island for nine years where he lived a hermit's life. He was invited back to Lindisfarne to become bishop, a position he held for two years before returning to Farne with a sense of impending death. He died

St. Cuthbert's viewed from Feetham's Field in the Thirties

there on Wednesday March 20, 687AD, and was buried on Lindisfarne. But the real story of St Cuthbert was only just beginning. From 793AD the Danes attacked the North of England, ravaging Lindisfarne. The monks fled, but when they realised they had left Cuthbert's body, returned to collect it. They disinterred it, packed it up in a wooden coffin with some old books, the head of the martyr King Oswald – the reason why statues depict St Cuthbert holding a spare head in his hand – who was also buried on Lindisfarne, and the remaining bones of St Aidan – some Scottish monks had removed much of their saint. On reaching the beach, the salvage party discovered the tide was unusually high and with the Danes at their backs prepared themselves for a long wait until they could get away.

But Cuthbert came to their rescue. In a scene straight out of The Bible the sea parted and the monks were able to walk across dry sand to reach dry land. As is often the case with such tales, their troubles were not over yet.

> *From Holy Ile,*
> *O'er northern mountain, marsh and moor,*
> *From sea to sea, from shore to shore,*
> *Seven years Saint Cuthbert's corpse they bore.*

The pillaging Danes were always on their trail, moving them on each time they settled. It seems unlikely that the monks actually set foot in Darlington on their travels – there wasn't much of the town built in those days – but they came quite close. Cotherston and Cowton are both corruptions of Cuthbert's town, which implies they found shelter there. The monks wandered around Cleveland and Yorkshire for a while, resting in Chester-le-Street in County Durham for a time until the Danes ejected them in 995AD. Following a brief time in Ripon they moved to Durham where they found a home.

Which brings the tale to somewhere between 1003 and 1016, when the earliest reference to the name Darlington is discovered. At a convention of worthies in York, a chap called Styr requested that he be allowed to give Dearningtun and its dependencies to Saint Cuthbert. King Ethelred the Unready, Archbishop Wulstan and Bishop Aldhume of Durham plus many other high-ranking personages of the realm agreed and solemnised the donation by putting a heavy curse on all who should violate the patrimony of the Saint.

Birds' Eye View

The copper weathercock has perched high above Darlington town centre at the top of St Cuthbert's Church spire for nearly 250 years. It first took to its place in 1746 but has been up and down many times since then. Four years later, the spire was struck by lightning and had to be rebuilt. In 1822, the weathercock was removed for repainting and then replaced only to be blown down by a high wind in November 1872. In 1931, the top part of the spire had to be rebuilt once more because the work of the 1750s was deteriorating. Again in 1960 the weathercock was on the ground receiving a coat of paint. The return of the weathercock to its perch on January 25 1873 following the storm moved one local resident with a poetical streak to put pen to paper and write an ode celebrating 50 years of achievement in Darlington since the bird was grounded in 1822.

> *Tis fifty springs since with golden wings*
> *I stood in our market square;*
> *The people cheered as my head I reared*
> *To crow in the high mid air.*
> *But the children then are now old grey men*
> *Who watched me on that day:*
> *O, who will live, an account to give,*
> *If to earth again I stray?*
> *The grand old spire they did admire*
> *When to my roost I flew*
> *And I've kept my stand high above the land*
> *With my weather eye in view.*

I've looked o'er my wings at wonderous things
Since George the Fourth did reign. [1]
I saw from my nest a wondrous guest
They called a railway train.
Fatigue it ne'er showed with its ponderous load
When down to the east it went;
Not a few exclaimed as it onward flamed
That the dark one evil meant.
Twas old number one went puffing along [2]
So smoothly o'er the rail,

And George from the North, who brought the thing forth,
Said truly it ne'er should fail. [3]
A man of fame with a princely name
I've seen the special bring
With power and might, his princely right
He swayed as Railway King. [4]
And his transient sway, though for a day
Was felt the nation o'er;
But now he's at rest where the painless breast
Can be disturbed no more.
And I have seen our glorious Queen
As on the line she hied
Give such a smile when for a while
My golden wings she spied. [5]
I remember well how the old church bell [6]
Rang loud for Sir Robert Peel [7]
As he rode with grace through the market place
To speak of the people's weal
And how the cheer went up so clear
When Kossuth came in sight: [8]
For, like a champion brave, he crossed the wave
To share in a Briton's right.
I saw from my stand, a sight most grand
As cheer on cheer rose high:
When thousands lined, and amply dined,
Off English beef and pie:
For old Earl Grey had swept away
The cobwebs of the past: [9]
And the great reform had passed the storm
And Britons freed at last.
Two gallant knights, for the people's rights

That year were save returned;
And the glowing fire of this southern shire
In Pease and Bowes still burned. [10]
I saw from my station a real corporation [11]
With councillors new from the mint
And I'm bound to believe that no burgess will grieve
If you give them a hint.
For a generous heart takes a noble part
In our honoured friend the Mayor [12]
And this good old town of Quaker reknown
Will his gifts most freely share.
From my stand on high my best I'll try
To tell how blows the wind;
And I humbly trust no sudden gust
Will prove to me unkind: [13]
For my body lay among the tombs one day
And I nearly had expired
But they brushed my comb and sent me home
To the place I most desired.'

J Horsley, February 1873

Notes:

1. George IV reigned from 1820-30. The weathercock was taken down for mending in 1822.
2. Locomotion Number One, the first engine on the Stockton and Darlington Railway which opened in 1825.
3. George Stephenson walked south from Newcastle to present his ideas for a railway to Edward Pease in Darlington.
4. George Hudson (1800-71) nicknamed 'The Railway King'. A rich man who played Edward Pease's role in bringing the railways to York, and was made Lord Mayor as a result. He helped finance many railways throughout the country until dishonest share dealings came to light. He was imprisoned in York Castle and died in London in comparative poverty two years before the poem was written.
5. Queen Victoria stopped in Darlington for 15 minutes on her way to Scotland on September 28, 1849. She also stopped at Bank Top on August 28 1851 when she was presented with a bouquet of flowers, and on August 30 1852 when she received a basket of fruit.
6. The old bell would refer to the four bells recast in 1775 and aug-

mented by two new bells. When St Cuthbert's Church was restored between 1862 and 1865 the bells were again recast. Two more bells given by Joseph Pease were added in 1866 .

7. Sir Robert Peel visited Darlington on September 1 1847. He addressed about 2,000 people from Central Hall, 'slightly partook of luncheon' before driving off in a carriage and four.

8. Lajos Kossuth was instrumental in the 1848 Hungarian revolution. When the uprising was crushed by the Austrian masters, Kossuth lived in exile in England touring and speaking.

9. On May 16 1832 a large public meeting in Darlington demanded that Earl Grey be made Prime Minister and that all public money be withheld from the Government until a Parliamentary Reform Act was passed that would satisfy the country. In June, with Grey at the helm, the Reform Act was passed, and a massive public dinner was held in Darlington market place on June 9 to celebrate.

10. The Reform Act divided County Durham into two constituencies and Darlington became the political metropolis of the southern division electing two MPs. In the 1832 election three candidates of a Liberal leaning stood. Joseph Pease junior polled 2,273 votes and John Bowes of Streatlam Castle polled 2,218. The unsuccessful man was Robert Duncomb Shafto of Whitworth who received 1,841 votes. Joseph Pease was the first Quaker to sit in the House of Commons. He attended the Coronation of Queen Victoria in 1837 dressed in the court costume of 'earlier Friends' – a fact that was remarked upon widely at the time in national newspapers and is regarded as being an important point on the road to religious toleration. Pease and Bowes were returned without opposition in 1835 and 1837. Pease retired in 1841 and was replaced by another liberal Lord Harry Vane, brother of the Duke of Cleveland. On his election campaign Bowes drove into Darlington accompanied by a band playing 'See the conquering hero comes'; 300 horsemen four abreast; a procession of carriages filled with voters decorated with blue and white rosettes and another 200 electors on horseback. He was introduced to the crowd by Pease outside the Sun Inn on the corner of Northgate and Bondgate. Pease spoke for 20 minutes, but his voice was drowned out by the hooting, roaring and bellowing crowd. Bowes spoke for 30 minutes but no-one heard him either. The crowd then hung about the market place until 7pm when a fight broke out over a rosette. Historian Longstaffe reported: 'The police interfered, and finding themselves, through their rashness, in an awkward dilemma, struck out, and one man, well known as a quiet inoffensive character of the name of Robson,

The view at the turn of the century with Stonebridge in the foreground. The buildings are where the ring road is now

a butcher in Skinnergate, was unluckily struck by a police trun-cheon, and for sometime it was thought he was killed.' All hell broke out, and the police were forced to flee in all directions, los-ing their hats and truncheons. Some of them took refuge in the Town hall which the mob attacked. By 11pm all the windows in the hall were smashed so the rioters forced their way into the municipal building. The imprisoned police were disguised and smuggled out the back, saving them from what Longstaffe feels would have been certain death. He wrote: 'The mob, finding that they had escaped, tore up the bar railings, broke the forms and chairs, and committed every kind of outrage.'

Satisfied they then went home, smashing the odd window on the way. But Bowes, who later founded The Bowes Museum, was elected with 2,483 votes. Vane polled 2,547. Unsuccessful in 1841 was James Farrer of Ingleborough, Yorkshire, who was a conser-vative. He received 1,739 votes, but when Bowes retired in 1847 having spent £30,000 contesting the seat, Farrer took his place.

11. Darlington was made a corporate town in 1867.

12. Alderman Luck was Mayor in 1873.

13. The weathercock was blown from its perch in November 1872 and replaced in February 1873.

HEADLAM HALL

HEADLAM, NR GAINFORD, DARLINGTON, COUNTY DURHAM DL2 3HA
TEL: 0325 730238 FAX: 0325 730790

This magnificent Jacobean mansion is set in 3 acres of formal gardens in quiet rural Teeside. Originally built in the 17th century, the hall was home for 150 years to the Brocket family and more recently to Lord Gainford. The grounds include a small private trout water enclosed by ancient yew and beech hedges. The hotel has a tennis court, croquet lawn, a new swimming pool, sauna, exercise area and snooker room. All the bedrooms are individually furnished, and the restaurant provides the best of traditional English cuisine. The main hall features a magnificent carved oak fireplace and open staircase, while the Georgian drawing room opens onto a stepped terrace overlooking the lawns. Fishing and golf are nearby and Barnard Castle and Durham are only a short drive away. Conferences for up to 40. Free bedroom and champagne breakfast are provided for newly weds holding their reception here. Closed over Christmas. Dogs by prior arrangement. Price guide: £55–£72. Directions: Headlam is 2 miles north of Gainford off the A67, Darlington to Barnard Castle.

Highcliff Design Ltd.

INDIVIDUAL BUILDING & JOINERY TO THE HIGHEST STANDARD

We wish continued success to Headlam Hall Hotel after our completion of conference facilities, pool and leisure complex, bedroom annexe and furnishing contracts

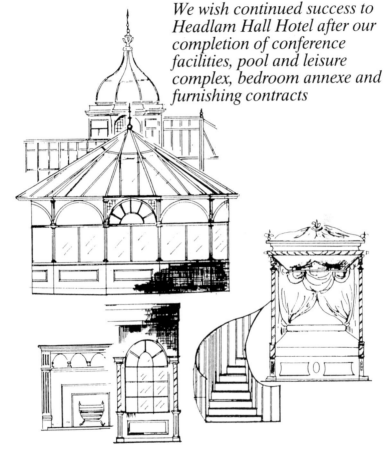

Highcliff Design Ltd.

COMPLETE BUILDING & JOINERY SERVICE INCLUDES:

- RESIDENTIAL AND COMMERCIAL BUILDING
- PROPERTY EXTENSIONS AND ALTERATIONS
- CUSTOM BUILT CONSERVATORIES
- WINDOW & BESPOKE JOINERY

- STAIRCASES
- SHOP FITTING & BAR FITTING
- PARTITIONS
- FURNITURE INCLUDING FOUR POSTER BEDS, FIRE SURROUNDS AND DRESSERS

FOR PERSONAL ATTENTION, ADVICE AND DESIGN CONSULT

DARLINGTON 0325 383587

WHESSOE ROAD, DARLINGTON DL3 0XL

Water Leisure Engineering Ltd

are pleased to be the insallers of the Leisure Pool at the Headlam Hall Hotel complex.

We offer the complete service for swimming pool owners from Hotel to Domestic installations.

Self-build kits also available.

For details regarding full range of services contact:

WATER LEISURE Engineering Ltd.

Fox Hall Cottage, East Layton, nr Richmond, North Yorkshire, DL11 7PW

C. & G.
MODEL RAILWAYS

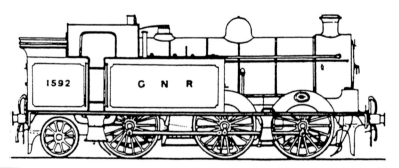

Stockists of All Leading Makes of 'N' and '00' Model Railways at Bargain Prices

LARGE STOCKS OF RAILWAY BOOKS AND STEAM AGE PHOTOGRAPHS

AHDQC   **Credit Cards Accepted**   44-260

CAPABILITY BROWNS

ROASTERS
TABLE

SUNDAY LUNCHES Only £8.50 Child £4.25

Complimentary Celebration Cakes for Parties or 4 or more

"The Best Joint in Town"
for you to carve in unlimited quantity

Little and Large — The choice is yours

From our Succulent Prime Roasts,
Beef, Lamb or Pork Salad Table
Vegetarian and a la carte menus also available

Open daily 12.30-1.45 and 7.00-9.45 p.m.

INTERNATIONAL HOTELIERS

CAPABILITY BROWN'S RESTAURANT

**Blackwell Grange Moat House, Blackwell Grange
Darlington, Co. Durham DL3 8QH**

AYDML *Table Reservations: (0325) 380888* 45-073

The Northern Echo

READER OFFER

North Country Walks 3
By Keith Watson

ONLY £4

A third super collection of 30 walks, from 4 to 12 miles, each with easy-to-follow maps and at-a-glance notes packed with painstaking detail and historical information. Stride out in the heart of North Country on a tour which takes in the wild coastline of Northumberland, spectacular Yorkshire Dales scenery and the mysterious Neolithic stone circles of Cumbria.

North Country Walks 3 is available at £4.00 each by calling at the following Northern Echo offices:
Priestgate, Darlington; 127 Newgate Street, Bishop Auckland; Saddler Street, Durham or 150 High Street, Northallerton.

Alternatively you can order the book by post. Simply complete the form below and send a cheque (made payable to North of England Newspapers) for £4.00 plus 75p postage and packing per copy to: North Country Walks Offer 3, The Northern Echo, Promotions Department, Priestgate, Darlington DL1 INF.

Name ....

Address ....

....

Postcode .... Tel. ....

Number of books required (at £4.00 + 75p per book) ....

Town Mansions

The prosperity brought to Darlington during the 19th century by the railways, ironworks and engineering industries enabled the magnates in charge to build for themselves gentrified mansions. As many of the captains of industry were members of the Pease family and so Quakers their villas were comfortable rather than the height of luxury. All the mansions were built in the countryside on the edge of the town. But as Darlington prospered so it grew, leaving the early halls stranded in what is now regarded as the town centre.

Jonathan Backhouse of Polam Hall

The man who started the upper-crust craze of mansion living was Jonathan Backhouse (1779-1842), pictured right. In 1825 he bought a modest house which the previous owner rather boastfully called Polam Hall. Within three years Jonathan had expanded Polam into the first presentable villa. The wealth required for such a ground-breaking project came largely from his father, also called Jonathan (1747-1826), who ran a highly successful enterprise that involved gold, forgery, execution and mad dashes from London to save the business. An imposing monument to the achievements of the family still stands in High Row. To this day townspeople refer to it as Backhouse's Bank even though it has had the name of Barclays above the door since 1896.

The Backhouses started their bank almost by accident in 1774. Jonathan senior and his father James were originally linen man-

81

Polam Hall pictured in 1857

ufacturers and as successful entrepreneurs often extended credit to the farmers and tradesmen they dealt with. These deals grew into a full-blown banking business which needed an office of its own. They took the lease on a shop in Northgate near the Crown Street corner, but after only five years they ran into trouble with a fraudulent forger. On October 3 1778 they issued a statement offering a £50 reward for information leading to the apprehension of a certain John Mathison of Gretna Green, Scotland. They claimed Mathison was behind the forging of five guinea notes apparently signed and so validated by James Backhouse himself. The statement read:

The said John Mathison is about 30 years of age, of a middle stature, and strong made though thin; his face a little marked with small-pox and one of his legs appears rather thicker at the ankle than the other, occasioned, it is supposed, by its having been broken some time ago; and speaks the Scotch dialect.

Realising his game was up, Mathison fled to London where he continued to perpetrate his crimes against the Bank of England. He changed his name to Maxwell and when he was arrested on suspicion of defrauding the Old Lady of Threadneedle Street there was not enough evidence to lock him up for good. Then the Backhouse statement was unearthed and it was put to him that his name was Mathison not Maxwell and it was suggested that he bore an uncanny resemblance to the Backhouse description. The master forger immediately broke down in tears sobbing: 'And now I will confess all'. He had been forging the notes of numerous provincial banks, he said, but in return for clemency he offered to divulge his secret method of copying watermarks. The police declined his offer. Mathison was tried, convicted, and sentenced to be hanged. His execution was carried out at Newgate Prison on July 28 1779. James Backhouse died nine years after the trial and the bank took the name of his son.

In 1815 another of Darlington's banks, Messrs Mowbray, Hollingsworth and Co, failed and the Backhouses picked up the pieces and moved into Mowbray's premises on High Row – where Barclays is today. The execution of Mathison did not signal the end of the bank's worries. Some time during the early 19th Century Harry Vane, Duke of Cleveland, also known as Earl of Darlington, bore a grudge against the Backhouses and set his mind on breaking the bank. His Lordship ordered that all his tenants must pay their rent with Backhouse notes. Once he had collected his dues he intended to present all the notes to the bank and demand gold in return – as was his right. He calculated that the Backhouses would not have enough bullion in their safes to pay up and so would be declared bankrupt and ruined. But he calculated without the resourcefulness of Jonathan Backhouse. Jonathan got wind of the nobleman's plans and managed to arrange a large supply of gold with the Royal Mint. The banker dashed down to London in his horse and carriage to get the stash. With His Lordship running around collecting notes, Jonathan thundered back up to Darlington to save the family bank. Disaster struck when he reached Croft and one of the wheels on his carriage fell off. Jonathan piled all of the heavy bullion on the opposite side of the coach to the broken wheel, balancing it out, and so was able to speed into Darlington. His Lordship's agent turned up at the bank and presented a large parcel of notes and demanded gold. The Backhouses calmly passed every ounce requested over the counter and as the bemused agent turned to leave, Jonathan said: 'Now tell thy master that if he will sell Raby Castle I will pay for it with the same metal.'

Jonathan seems to have been a character. His favourite pub trick was to burn money. He was a regular at the Kings Head in Barnard Castle where he would show his indifference to material wealth by tossing £5 notes onto the fire. In one version of the story, a traveller in the pub boasting about the size of his roll of bank notes challenged Backhouse over who had the most cash. The Quaker Backhouse would not rise to the bet but did offer to burn a note on the fire if the stranger would also do so. Not to be out-done, the stranger took up the challenge at which point Jonathan thanked him and pointed out he had now lost his entitlement to five pounds of gold whereas he, the bank owner, had simply lost a piece of paper.

The rather austere building still standing in High Row was opened in 1866. The Backhouses had the former Mowbray and Hollingsworth building pulled down in 1864 and asked fellow Quaker Alfred Waterhouse to draw up the new design. The name Barclays came into being in 1896 when 20 provincial banks, including Backhouse's, decided to increase their strength by amalgamating.

If the High Row bank is a monument to Jonathan senior so Polam Hall is a monument to his son Jonathan junior. The word 'polam' had long been applied to the low-lying marshy areas along the banks of the wide Skerne. It could have its derivation from an Anglo-Saxon word 'polum' meaning pools. By the 15th Century it had become Polinpole or Polum-pole, and by Tudor times it had evolved into Polham or Polam. Until 1729 Polam was part of the pinder's land – the pinder being the man who looked after stray animals. It was then gradually sold off and by the end of the 18th Century there was High Polam, Little Polam, Polam Green and Powlam Park Farm dotted on both sides of the Skerne in the area.

In 1794 a linen merchant, Harrington Lee, took over part of the land near Grange Road and started building a 'small villa' – a derisory term applied about 50 years later by those who had built more ostentatious mansions in other parts of the town. It was the first time in Darlington's social history that a man of means had decided to build himself a residence just outside the town centre in the countryside. Lee's drapery shop was above what eventually became an ice-cream parlour in Horsemarket near the Bull Wynd entrance. When he started building work on Polam Darlington's population was just 5,000 and there were only about 500 houses. Lee continued this theme of over-population. He was aged 27 when he moved into the house with four ground floor rooms with his wife Margaret and their 16 children. The family lived there for about 25 years until there was simply no more room when they moved out towards Coniscliffe.

In the meantime Jonathan Backhouse junior was buying up the surrounding farms with Polam in their name, building himself a tiny empire. When Lee died in 1824 his Polam Hall was the final piece in Backhouse's jigsaw. It took him three years to develop Lee's hall into a residence suitable for his wife, Hannah, and their four surviving children. As well as enlarging the original beyond recognition – although much of the 1794 building still remains – Backhouse laid out 36 acres of gardens, shrubberies and plantations with a large fishpond at the centre. Hannah was not over-impressed by the comparative luxury. In 1830 she felt called to the ministry and for five years she toured America, often enduring great hardships while spreading the word. When she returned to her husband she still felt awkward in the hall, and so when letter writing she put her address as Polam Hill which sounds a little less grand. Jonathan Backhouse died in 1842. His one surviving son Edmund moved into Polam Hall until 1848. Hannah died in 1850 leaving the mansion vacant.

But there were ready-made tenants in the form of the Misses Proctor: Jane, Barbara and Elizabeth of Selby who were related to the Pease family. In 1848 they founded a boarding school in Houndgate, principally for daughters of Quakers, and a couple of years later they set up in the hall. They were stern ladies, involved in the Temperance movement through which they knew the original Thomas Cook who arranged excursions to Scotland for their pupils. Jane was the last of the sisters to die in 1882, and the school floundered and closed for a while before in 1888 the Lockwoods brought their charges from Kendal and restarted the seat of education with 11 pupils.

Sir David Dale of West Lodge

West Lodge also owes its existence to the Backhouse family. Jonathan Backhouse senior's father James started work at the lodge in the late 18th Century when he moved into Darlington from Lancashire as an executive in his father-in-law's linen business. When James died in 1798 his nephew Thomas took over and West Lodge became known for a while as Killy Cat Hall. Thomas had left the States at the time of the Revolution and so was nicknamed Mercian or American Backhouse. Untypically for the staunch Quaker family he was a huntsman. He kept dogs and bred rabbits which apparently over-ran the gardens.

But he did build a new front on the house in 1803 and added two single-storey wings which have since been demolished. On Thomas's death in 1824 his cousin Jonathon took up residence for a couple of years, before passing West Lodge on to his son James. James junior built the Swiss Cottage that was demolished to allow the Memorial Hospital to expand in the Seventies. James junior passed away in 1837 and West Lodge passed on to his sister Ann who pushed it on in

1852 to her married sister Jane Robson. In turn Jane bequeathed the home to her daughter Ann Backhouse Robson who married the industrialist David Dale, pictured below. Until his death in 1906 Dale spent much money improving the building and its gardens.

Dale was born in 1829 in India where his father was with the East India Company. Mr Dale senior died on board ship in 1830 as the family was returning home to Scotland. Without the head of the family to protect them, the three young Dales and their mother caught a mail coach to Glasgow. Nearing Darlington a serious accident befell the coach and Mrs Dale was so severely injured she had to be carried to the Kings Head Hotel. Such was the kindness shown to her by the Quakers in the town during her hour of need that Mrs Dale decided to return to Darlington and make a permanent home there. One accident lured David Dale to Darlington and another drew him to West Lodge. In 1853 he married Mrs Ann Whitwell whose first husband, Henry, had been mistakenly shot during a disturbance in Madrid five years earlier. Before she wed Mrs Whitwell was Miss Ann Backhouse Robson, grand-daughter of Jonathon Backhouse senior, and with her second husband she lived in the family home at West Lodge. At the time of his marriage Dale, who had business connections with the Pease family, was steadily working his way up through the ranks of the various railway administrations in the area until he went into partnership with W Bouch, building railway engines in Shildon. When the Shildon shops became too small the partnership moved to Darlington and installed itself in the North Road Shops. The first engine made there was called Contractor after Dale himself.

In 1864 he formed another partnership with Joseph Whitwell Pease and bought up the ailing Consett Iron Works for £295,000. Dale is credited with turning the foundry into a palace of industry and he held the chairmanship from 1884 until his death. It was during the troubled late 1860s and 1870s that he made an international name for himself. Industrial unrest was widespread and apart from 'barbarous, cruel and stupid' strikes and lockouts there was no way of dealing with disputes. In 1869 Dale was made the first president of the Board of Arbitration and Conciliation for the iron

Tennis on the lawn at West Lodge

trade manufacturers of the North of England. Its first meeting was held in March 1869 in Central Hall and brought the warring sides together for discussion. His expertise in this field of industrial relations took him all over Europe – he was in Germany in 1870 when the Franco-Prussian War broke out.

On a parochial level Dale was equally active, taking particular interest in education. He was a governor of the former Grammar School in Darlington. Being a Quaker at this stage of his life he was also involved in Liberal politics. But despite requests to stand for Parliament in at least eight North-East seats he declined to enter the national political arena. One Darlington Liberal was so keen on his nomination he penned the following verse:

> *Yes Dale shall be the people's choice*
> *In some fair Liberal City near,*
> *When Liberal hearts will all rejoice*
> *To welcome one without a Peer.*

Such was Dale's involvement in so many causes and organisations his mother's last words on her deathbed shortly before Christmas 1879 were said to have been: 'Pray for my son in the midst of his many pressing engagements'. His wife died in 1886, and two years later he married the elder daughter of Sir Frederick Milbank of Barningham Hall. A special train was laid on to take guests from Darlington to the church in Bedale. His second marriage also marked the beginning of his turning away from the Society of Friends and he became a frequent worshipper at Holy Trinity Church.

In 1895 Queen Victoria accepted Prime Minister Lord Rosebery's advice and conferred a knighthood on Dale. The people of Darlington, his adopted home town, were so impressed there was talk of making him the first freeman of the borough, but the matter was for some reason forgotten. His knighthood and international reputation did not prevent a scandal at West Lodge, the scene of many top level international conferences. In 1903 his butler made off with a large quantity of precious silverware. Much of the loot was discovered in local pawnshops but Sir David found to his horror that the trusty butler had been syphoning off his valuables for several months. The butler was jailed for six months and the magistrates censured the pawnbrokers.

Perhaps it was predictable that a man who had come to Darlington by accident should suffer an unusual death. Sir David had been unwell for a couple of years when on April 28 1906 he insisted on fulfilling his meetings in London and then returning by train to Darlington. As it neared Grantham he was taken seriously ill. A London doctor battled to save him but by the time the train reached York he had to be carried off to the Station Hotel where he died of heart trouble. Remembering the stolid service he had given to the railway industry a special train was laid on that day to transport his remains home to West Lodge. In his will he left £121,000 and he is buried in West Cemetery.

After Dale West Lodge was bought by builder Ralph Blackett – the Bondgate pub still bears his name – appropriate as Blackett had built the North Road Shops for the industrialist. And Blackett was also responsible for the break-up of the estate as his firm built West Crescent. It did a similar job on the Pierremont estate. Blackett sold the Lodge to John Henry Roberts, owner of the Northgate Steel Wire Mills in John Street, who had made a bomb out of the war effort. Roberts lost much of his money on a property deal in Morecambe and had to sell up in 1926. Two years later West Lodge was turned over to its current use as a home for community organisations.

Francis Mewburn of Larchfield

A third mansion which has Backhouse connections stood on the site of the St Augustine's church centre on the corner of Larchfield Street and Coniscliffe Road. Back when time began this part of Darlington was a field called Lambs Flatts. Therefore when John Backhouse, the younger brother of Jonathan Backhouse of Polam Hall, built the mansion in 1811 it was called Lamb Flatt House. John changed the mansion's name from Lamb Flatt to Paradise in the mid-1820s. The house had one-and-three-quarter acres of well-established gardens and as the century progressed various extensions were added to the basic four-room design. In 1831 solicitor Francis Mewburn, pictured left, took up residence and changed the name to Larchfield. He is supposed to have been told that no solicitor could ever live in paradise. Mewburn styled himself the First Railway Solicitor. He was the last chief citizen of Darlington, the last Chief Bailiff of the Bishop's Borough and, according to Joseph Pease, was a man with the heart of a chicken. Francis, who was born in Bishop Middleham in November 1785, was the legal advisor to Edward Pease, father of the railways, and George Stephenson, designer of the railways. He came to Darlington in May 1809. In 1811 he founded the Darlington Society for the Prosecution of Felons and for two years ran a school for poor children in St Cuthbert's Church.

He became involved early on in the Quaker project to get the railways moving even though he was of the Church of England persuasion and a regular worshipper at Holy Trinity Church. A stained glass window in St Cuthbert's commemorates him and includes figures of St Andrew and St Barnabas – he was born and died on these saints' days. The Mewburn family motto was 'Festina lente'. Translated from the Latin this means 'Hasten with caution' and it was this deliberation that annoyed Joseph Pease who said: 'Francis Mewburn, if I had no more courage than thee, I should do nothing at all; thou has the heart of a chicken. I am determined to try out the railway.' Caution gave way to Pease's haste, and Mewburn soon became keen on the idea. At a luncheon to celebrate the opening of the railway in 1829 from Croft to Haughton Road he astounded guests by prophesying that in a few years train travellers would leave Darlington in the morning, attend the opera in London in the evening and return to Darlington the following morning in time for breakfast.

Pease obviously trusted Mewburn. When the Quaker was first elected to parliament in 1833 he took the solicitor to London with him to negotiate with the speaker of the Commons an oath acceptable to all parties. In November 1846 Bishop Maltby appointed Mewburn Chief Bailiff of Darlington to act as the Bishop's manager in the town. It was a prestigious position and as there was no mayor he was regarded as the town's chief citizen – and when he died the post died with him. Even before this honour was bestowed upon him – it earned him £5 a year plus the rent of a field at Dodmire – Mewburn was so highly thought of he was often asked to perform mayoral functions. On July 6 1824 he laid the foundation stone of the Skerne Railway Bridge and on June 5 1832 he performed a similar duty when work began on Blackwell Bridge. When Queen Victoria came visiting on September 28 1849 it was Mewburn who presented the address of loyalty at Bank Top station. The Mewburn clan – in 1850 the 65-year-old Francis was living there with his wife Elizabeth, seven children and four servants – stayed at Larchfield until Elizabeth died at the age of 93 in 1884. She outlived her husband by 17 years. From the 1920s a Roman Catholic Girls' School held lessons in its rooms until the reorganisation of education in 1975. Lamb Flatt House or Paradise or Larchfield or Carmel School was demolished in 1978.

Joseph Pease of Southend

Southend was the home of Darlington's most famous son, Joseph Pease, pictured left, born on June 22, 1799. But it started life in the all-pervading Backhouse family. It is now the Grange Hotel but when banker Edward built the plain brick hall at the start of the 19th Century he called it Borrowses or Burrows – a name derived from the fields on which it was built on the edge of the borough. In 1826 Joseph Pease (1799-1872) took over and substantially enlarged both the house and the gardens. His estate eventually included the Harewood area and Green

Southend pictured in 1890

Park and there were stables along Coniscliffe Road. Joseph's statue stands in High Row and attracts much attention from weekend drinkers who delight in festooning it with a variety of stolen items, but in his day Joseph attracted national attention as a mould-breaker. He effectively founded Middlesbrough, was involved with the Stockton and Darlington Railway, became the largest coal-owner in the North-East, gave Darlington South Park and was the first Quaker MP. He entered the House of Commons on February 8 1833, the first person to represent the constituency of South Durham which had been created with Darlington at its centre by the Great Reform Act of 1831. To the annoyance of the clergy and local gentry he was persuaded by those of a Liberal inclination to stand for Parliament and was elected with a majority of 55. His decision to enter the political arena angered the Quaker community in which Edward, his father who is also tagged the father of the railways, was a leading light. In a letter Joseph says of Edward's opposition: 'He expressed his decided opinion that unless I was wholly regardless of all parental council, the advice of all my best friends, the domestic happiness of my family, my

The boathouse at Southend and, below, inside Southend. Both pictures from 1890

duties as a husband and a parent, and a member of the Society of Friends, I could not for a moment entertain the idea of yielding under any contingency to represent my countrymen in Parliament.'

He obviously was regardless of all these things because he went through with the dastardly deed, although he promised his mother-in-law there would be no 'image selling' for him.

In another letter he says: 'I will not canvass. I will not ask one man for his vote. I will go to no expense. I will, both in and out of Parliament, unflinchingly support my practice and my profession as a member of the Society of Friends.'

Getting to the door of the House meant overcoming many obstacles; on getting through it he was presented with another set. He was proffered the printed forms with the oath all MPs had to swear before taking their seats. Because of his religious convictions he refused to take it, and a constitutional crisis was at hand. The Prime Minister immediately set up a working party to sort out the matter and Pease's supporters urged him to petition Parliament.

Said Joseph: 'I will petition nobody. I was sent here according to the law of the land as representative in Parliament for South Durham, an important county constituency, and it shall never be said that South Durham in my person was brought down upon its knees to beg for its rights.'

A week later and the PM's working party reported that Joseph could take his seat, and he became a national hero – the first Puritan MP since the time of the Commonwealth. Being a Quaker meant having a strict standard of dress which kept him in the public eye. It also troubled Pease as he found himself in danger of breaking the Quaker's 'hat testimony'.

At Queen Victoria's coronation in 1837 his presence was remarked upon as if he were a dignitary from a foreign land:

> *Then the noble Prussians, likewise the Russians. And the Bavarians and the proud Hungarians. Then Misthur Spaker with Misthur Pays, the Quaker.*

Irish politicians did not take so kindly to him, especially when in his usual straightforward style he accused them of duplicity. The MP for Drogheda, a Mr Dwyer, sent him a formal challenge to a duel, extending him the choice of weapons. Joseph quietly ignored it. He continued his work in the North-East in the fields of business and benevolence. He bought and leased more coal-fields than anyone else, using the family railway to transport the minerals cheaply. Realising the need for a port to assist with exports he bought 521 acres of land on the Tees from which Middlesbrough grew. He helped the fledgling town by setting up about 20 schools, and in his home-town he paid for South Park and St Cuthbert's Church cemetery to be laid out.

He donated the town clock, eight drinking fountains and a steam fire-engine. The Spanish Government awarded him the Order of the Grand Cross of Charles III for donating books to them shortly before he died at home in Southend on February 8, 1872. He had been blind for seven years and it was estimated that 10,000 men were employed in his industries. His personal property was valued at £350,000. The High Row monument, paid for by public subscription, was unveiled in 1875 as part of the 50th celebration of the Stockton and Darlington railway. It is very doubtful that the great Quaker would have much time for the drunkards who now periodically defile it. In his pamphlet Hints for the Working Man he says: 'The man that stupifies himself with tobacco and besots himself with drink is not likely to make much progress in education. Drink fills the workhouses, gaols and asylums, gives work at the Assizes and leads to poverty and misery. I pity the publican and his wife. I weep when I see a family taking over a public house. Their history is a catalogue of woes. The charm of the women is defaced and the strong men are hurried to an untimely grave.'

When he died his unmarried daughters Emma and Jane continued to live in Southend until they passed away at the turn of the century. The Southend Estate Company moved in and built Southend Avenue and Oakdene Avenue over much of the gardens, and Beechwood Avenue is on the site of the large fish pond.

Darlington Corporation took over the belt of trees alongside Grange Road and developed the Rookery as a public garden filled with crocuses. This was formally opened in 1901. The mansion became a Roman Catholic School for girls run by the Sisters of St Vincent de Paul and dormitories were added in 1905 on the Coniscliffe Road side. The stables were converted into a school chapel. In the late Seventies the school moved to Hummersknott, and the hotel took over.

Joseph Whitwell Pease of Woodlands

Tucked away behind the petrol station on Woodland Road, Darlington, is the 13-bedroomed stately home which has been described as 'the jewel in Darlington's crown'. It is thought work was started on this mansion in 1815 by Robert Botcherby, a timber merchant, for his own use. He stayed until his sudden death in 1838. For nearly 20 years a number of moderately important people lived there

Joseph Whitwell Pease (1828-1903) pictured with, from left, Sarah Charlotte Hodgkin, (born 1858) Maud Mary Pease (1862) Mrs Helen Blanche Pease (1865) Lucy Ethel Buxton (1867) and Agnes Claudia Fox Wilson (1870)

until the big one came along in 1854 in the shape of Sir Joseph Whitwell Pease MP. Sir Joseph was born on June 23, 1828, at Southend, Darlington, the eldest son of Joseph Pease. At the age of 17 he enlisted in his family's enormous business empire and quickly became an important figure developing mines all over the North-East and building railways to serve them. He was instrumental in creating the Barnard Castle branch-line from Darlington. He came to the House of Commons in 1865 representing South Durham – the same constituency his father had retired from in 1841. When political boundaries were redrawn in 1885, he chose the Barnard Castle area of the South Durham constituency as his own and was always re-elected as a Liberal without too much trouble. Sir Joseph was given a baronetcy in 1882 and was a foremost campaigner against the opium trade between India and China. As President of the Peace Society he was a firm advocate of international arbitration as opposed to the arbitration of the sword.

In December 1902 the family bank, J and W Pease of Darlington, crashed. It was an exclusive bank where account holders had to be members of the Pease family. A few leading companies in the North of England were also allowed to use the bank's services – many of these companies were owned by the family. So when J and W Pease crashed, much of the strength of the Pease empire went down too – including Sir Joseph, who died six months later. His body was transported from Falmouth in Cornwall to Woodside in Darlington, the home of his sister-in-law, Mrs Gurney Pease. Anyone who was anyone attended the funeral in the Friends Meeting House in Skinnergate. After his death the predictable sympathies were trotted out but perhaps the most poignant came from the Darlington Trades Council. Under the presidency of Geoffrey Beeton the council said it was deeply grieved to hear the news of Sir Joseph, not only of his death: 'But also at the great misfortunes that had overtaken him in the later days of his life after a career spent in hard, laborious work. Though not a manual worker perhaps Sir Joseph worked a great deal harder than many working men. It was evidence that it was not only the workman who was a victim of the present system under which he lived for Sir Joseph was one of the last we would have thought would succumb to financial troubles. It seemed to be a sad end to a long and useful life.'

At the time of his death Sir Joseph was the Father of the House as he was the longest serving member of the Commons. Even so in 1902 he said: 'To this moment it is a most uncomfortable place to speak in.' Sir Joseph resided in Woodlands for just seven years before moving to Hutton Hall in Guisborough which was designed for him by Alfred

Waterhouse. But in that time he doubled the size of the house. The most noticeable of his improvements is the imposing tower.

After Sir Joseph's term of residence more moderately top-notch people lived in Woodlands, including wine merchant Thomas Plews and his eight children, five staff and wife. In 1908 much of the estate was sold for building and the original coach house now has the petrol station standing on it.

Arthur Pease of Hummersknott

A hummer is a grassy slope down to a river and a knott is a bump on a hillside. When they come together they produce Hummersknott, the idyllic site for one of Darlington's more famed nineteenth century mansions. 'The view from Windsor Castle is deservedly esteemed, but it is tame and flat compared with that from Hummersknott. The whole of the Tees Valley, from the purple mosses of Stainmore to the wooden heights of Richmond, lie in one's gaze.' Such was an anonymous poetic writer's description of the belle vue in 1877.

Arthur Pease

Hummersknott Villa was built in 1864 by Joseph Pease of Southend for his third son, Arthur, pictured left, left home in April of that year when he married Mary Lecky Pike. He was Mayor of the town in 1873-4 and served continuously on the council for 31 years. He was elected as a Unionist to the House of Commons in 1895 – three years before his death. To mark his year as Mayor, Arthur, who was president of the local Temperance Association, built a large hotel in Grange Road which he called The Trevelyan Temperance Hotel. The name was no longer applicable when in 1892 Edward Wooler took over and obtained an intoxicating liquor licence, so it was changed to The Imperial Hotel. Arthur was also president of the South Durham and North Yorkshire Horse and Dog Show and in that capacity he was able to attract the Royal Agricultural Society Show to his

Hummersknott, Darlington, drawn when the Royal Agricultural Show was held there

260-acre park, the first royal show ever to be held in County Durham. More than 100,000 people flocked to the week-long show, including the Duke and Duchess of York, the Shah of Persia and his Highness the Shahzada of Afghanistan. Arthur died three years after the show. His son, Herbert Pike Pease who was born at Hummersknott, succeeded to the mansion and to his father's seat in the Commons.

The writing was on the wall for the estate as early as 1858 when Arthur started the break-up by donating 12 acres of land to the town to make West Cemetery. By 1927 it was being divided and put up for sale, described in the estate agents' blurb as 'probably the most attractive and desirable building estate which has ever been offered locally'. The other important houses, Uplands and Tees Grange, which were on the Hummersknott land as it stretched from Nunnery Lane to Coniscliffe Road, have been demolished and built on – although Wilton House is now a residential home. Hummersknott itself has fared a little better. After the Army used it as a camp during World War One, the Roman Catholic authorities acquired it in 1930 and transformed it into St Mary's Grammar School. Arthur's home is now almost completely surrounded by school buildings.

120 YEARS OF QUALITY
ZISSLER & SONS

The Founders:
George Christian and Magdelina Regina Zissler

The Present:
Paul Victor and Sue Zissler

For four generations 'The Old Firm' has been manufacturing
quality traditional pork products daily at:

104 BONDGATE, DARLINGTON

BEJNL

50-260

North of England Newspapers
Limited Edition Print Offer

Durham Cathedral

Barnard Castle

Fountains Abbey

York Minster

LIMITED EDITION OF 300 PAIRS-ONLY £29.99 EACH PLUS DELIVERY

North of England Newspapers are delighted to offer readers the unique opportunity to purchase a pair of beautiful limited edition (only 300 pairs per set) colour prints.

The first pair feature York Minster and Fountains Abbey ruins. The second Durham Cathedral and Barnard Castle.

Both sets of prints will arrive personally signed and numbered by the artist, David Coates and mounted in superb quality frames.

We can offer you the opportunity to purchase a pair for only £29.99, plus £2.51 delivery. Or both pairs at £59.98 plus £2.51 delivery.

To order, simply complete the panel below and post it to: Print Offer, The Promotions Dept., North of England Newspapers, Priestgate Darlington, Co. Durham, DL1 1NF.

Name ....

Address ....

....

Postcode .... Tel. ....

I wish to order: a ..... pairs of York Minster/Fountains Abbey; b ..... pairs of Durham Cathedral/Barnard Castle. I have enclosed a cheque/PO made payable to Concept Arts for £29.99 plus £2.51 or £59.98 plus £2.51 for the full set of prints.

100

Transport Delights

As everyone knows Darlington is the home, and quite possibly the birthplace, of the railways. Running on a different track Darlington was the first town in the North-East to have a tram system. The Darlington Street Railroad Company started operation on January 1, 1862. From the south end of town to the North Road railway station it ran two cars patriotically named Nelson and Wellington. The system was designed with help from Birkenhead experts who had opened the first streetcar network in the country two years earlier. In turn, they had been briefed by American George Francis Train, who owned the patent following his innovative work on the first tram line in the world – the New York to Harlem street railway. In Darlington trams ran every ten minutes in both directions, starting at 8am and finishing at 8.10pm – 8.50pm on Saturdays. A journey cost 2d a head, but bargain bags of oval-shaped brass tokens could be bought. The town's engineers ran a lucrative sideline making imitations of these tokens.

The network ran into immediate problems – from cows and farmers. On January 18 1862, the Darlington and Stockton Times reported that 3,000 passengers had already made journeys, but the timetables were running late because of 'farmers' conveyances standing on the rails in Northgate for the greater part of the day'. Herds of cows being driven into market were also reluctant to get out of the way. The Darlington Street Railroad Company folded in 1865. It was already in financial difficulties – perhaps due to the forging – when a prize greyhound was run over and the compensation claim was too much for its coffers to bear.

Horses took over from steam. The town's main omnibus was pulled by three beasts from Blackwellgate to North Road station. The 19 passengers on the inside paid 3d and the 22 outside 2d. In October 1880 there was another attempt at streetcars, this time run by the Stockton and Darlington Steam Tramways Company. It owned 12 cars, although ran only seven at any one time on its 2.5 miles of 3ft track. Despite the company's name, the cars, which weighed up to five tons when empty, were pulled on rails by one or two horses depending on their size. There were two tramway lines but the North Road station to Feethams and Victoria Road track was closed in 1885. The other from the Market Place out to Cockerton continued to operate, and charged passengers 1d a mile. Horses were replaced after 15 miles, which works out at about eight return trips. In January 1902 the council decided it was time for electrification and bought the network for £7,000. The council's Gas, Electricity and Transport Department leased it out to entrepreneur C. J. O'Dowd, and the last horse-drawn tram was in August 1903.

Mr O'Dowd began laying five miles of electrical track that converged on Prebend Row. Sixteen single deck trucks with the drivers in an open cab exposed to the weather were bought. The new system was opened on June 1, 1904 by MP and Mayor Arthur Henderson. His wife, the Mayoress, was allowed to drive the first car. The venture was well received by the townspeople and the corporation soon owned 24 blue and white cars.

But The First World War dealt a severe blow to the network and despite faster Straker-Clough trolley buses introduced in December 1925, on April 10, 1926 it was closed down. Darlington had lead the way in the North-East with the tram systems and so it was responsible for pioneering the trams' replacement: trolley buses. The first circular trolley route was opened on March 25 1928. It started at the Midland Bank, Northgate, and went up Station Road, Surtees Street and Willow Road to West Auckland Road. There were 24 trolleys at the start but the town soon augmented its fleet of Straker-Cloughs, Ransomes and English Electrics with 20 new Leylands. These new buses came with an added luxury: pnuematic tyres, and in 1929 all trolleys in the town had their hard wheels replaced. Even so the journeys were still liable to be bumpy as it was many years before the tram tracks were removed from the roads.

When the restrictions of The Second World War began to bite, Darlington had to take delivery of 16 austerity buses. They came in 1942 painted a suitable dull battleship grey. They had cane seats, although some were later fitted with cushions, and had ugly resistance boxes on their roofs. Double deckers emerged on the scene when the war was over. Being taller, there were new problems. North Road bridge was too low and it was decided to lower the road to allow them underneath. Even now a puddle of water sometimes collects in this unnatural dip.

The First World War had dealt a severe blow to the tram network and that never recovered, and similarly The Second World War sent

Trolley buses in Woodland Road, Darlington, in the Twenties

the trolley buses reeling. Darlington had 60 cars, but most of them were literally on their last wheels. The football club requested that extra buses be laid on to take the fans home after the match, but bus bosses had to turn this idea down because when two or three buses came to a stop the ageing electrical system had difficulty getting them moving again. So in 1946 the council decided to scrap the scheme altogether and an order for six new trolleys was cancelled. In 1947 the Ministry of Transport announced it would set up the British Transport Committee to supervise the nationalisation of local transport and told the council not to make any drastic changes to its network.

The council decided that scrapping trolley buses was a drastic change and reprieved the service. Six new trolleys were ordered. The new trolleys meant there were now 66 in the fleet, although it was rather bizarre that the last two were numbered 68 and 73. By 1947 trolleys were running alongside motorised vehicles. Darlington had had a brief flirtation with petrol-power as early as January 8, 1927 – before the inauguration of the trolleys – when four buses were hired. They did their job adequately, but passenger-power ended their com-

TELEPHONE 369   TELEGRAMS AUTOMOBILE DARLINGTON

Cleveland Car Co., Ltd., Darlington.

▲▲▲

Motor
Outings
of Any
Distance
Quoted for.

Open Cars,
Limousines
and
Landaulettes
for Hire.

The above CHAR-A-BANC will run, weather and circumstances permitting, on

To   **Return Fare**

Starting from

Seating accommodation for **18** Passengers.

It is to be understood that this Motor does not run unless there are 14 or more passengers.

Above: An early advert for the Cleveland Car Co. charabanc
Below: A United bus in 1924

Old and new United buses pictured in 1955

mercial life when the council was flooded by complaints about their comfort. Firms like the Cleveland Car Company were running out of town charabancs. The nationalisation committee decided enough was enough and called time on the trolleys. A gradual introduction of diesel buses was announced. Buses sped at 10mph compared with the trolleys' slovenly 8.5mph, although one trolley driver boasted about doing the Market Place to Haughton Green run in four minutes on a good day. The six double decker buses were sold off to Doncaster for £17,433 and ironically were still working well into the Sixties. In Darlington the last trolley trip was July 31, 1957 and the network was dismantled by June 4, 1958.

The Doncaster double deckers had now moved on to Bradford where in 1959 they came into contact with parts of the defunct Darlington electrical system. Since 1957, buses have monopolised the streets of Darlington. Originally they were painted deep blue, but the council changed that to cream with the coat of arms. Conductors with revolutionary ticket machines were introduced and then gradually phased out in favour of the one man mobiles.

A Horse Called Spider

The rich and famous were drawn from all over the world to the 189 agricultural show held in the splendid grounds of Hummersknott. Bu among the royalty and foreign rulers roamed Spider who, probabl unbeknown to the 100,000 crowd, was the real star of the show.

Spider was an eight-year-old black Dales pony bought just a wee before the show by Demer's the Darlington greengrocers. Spider' brief was to earn extra money with 13-year-old Charles Demer at the reins, transporting the visitors from Bank Top Station to Hummer sknott.

Business went well for the pair on the first day, but on the Tues day a horrendous thunderstorm broke over the showground. Spider and Charlie were out in the open as the rain pelted down, standing 2(yards from a large tree under which two men sheltered. Suddenl there was a sharp flash of lightning followed immediately by a lou(crash of thunder. When the smoke cleared, the two men lay dea(beneath the branches and Spider was reduced to a quivering wreck.

But ol' Mr Demer would have none of the nag's horseplay an(instructed young Charlie to take Spider to the Bull's Head pub in th(Market Place for a pint of ale slops. And Spider lapped it up and trun dled up to Bank Top to collect more passengers. He did 16 or 17 trip a day, but would only make a journey if he had a pint first in th(Bull's Head.

By the end of each day Spider had swilled nearly 20 pints. Th(landlord charged him 6d a drink, and Charlie collected 2s 6d fron each of the five passengers who boarded the tipsy taxi.

It is not recorded if Spider became an old soak. But we do know h(lived to the grand old age of 29, so the ale can't have done him any harm.

———— Ghost Stories ————

Ghosts, sprites and spirits abound in the Darlington area although it may only be coincidence that the incidence of spooky sightings has dramatically fallen off since the introduction of street lighting.

The Horror of Stephen Hollin

The Darlington and Stockton Times in 1883 records this story although even then the unnamed correspondent – presumably a ghostwriter – said Stephen, a farmer living alone in a desolate farmhouse on the wild carrs to the east of Manfield, was murdered a long time ago. But the writer was hopeful that he would put in an appearance in the near future as a priest exorcised his spirit for a period of years that was coming to an end. Stephen's death is cloaked in obscurity, but the legends agree he was murdered by two scheming nephews who had 'motives of cupidity'. They buried his body, but soon dug it up and burnt it in a brick oven after reports of his apparition as a ghost had made the local people suspicious. Everyone who saw the ghost agreed he was a short, thin man, with a face spotted with blood, wearing a brown coat, and low crowned hat. Sometimes he rode a grey horse; sometimes he was on foot. He always appeared within a mile of his isolated cottage called Cawd Knockles. According to the legend a farmhand from another lonely house dared to doubt the danger of trespassing through Stephen's territory in the dark.

'He cared now't for Awd Stephen, if he seed him he'd thraw't plough cowter at his heed,' said the locals of the hand's foolhardiness. The hand set off, only to be found dead next morning, his body scratched and torn as if he had been dragged over the fields and through the hedges. Generally, Stephen was a friendly ghost who caught runaway horses, helped with threshing corn and helped girls carry heavy pails of milk. Once he stole all the thread from a tailor and hid a newly-born calf in a tree. A local priest ended his tricks and 'conjured' him away. No-one has heard of him since.

Tragic Lady Jarratt

Lady Jarratt – Jarrett or Gerrard – is Darlington's most famous ghost although she has not been seen for over a century. She met her bloody end gallantly fighting off marauding Civil War soldiers at the Bishop's Palace. They burst into her room demanding money. She refused, but they noticed the expensive ring on her finger. One of the men held her prisoner and roughly covered her mouth to stifle her terrified screams. The other wrenched at her hand, but the gold ring stubbornly refused to budge. The frenzied soldier drew his sword and savagely hacked off her left arm, and the two plunderers made off with the rich pickings. Lady Jarratt stumbled to the wall and sank lifeless to the floor, her blood-stained right hand leaving a deep crimson mark as she fell. Legend has it that that mark was immoveable, no matter how hard the wall was scrubbed. As the poet says:

'This Lady who in violence died,
Left her blood, that none could hide,
Her desolate vigil, still to keep,
While Darlington folk are sound asleep.'

Lady Jarratt was believed to traverse every night a subterranean passage leading from the Palace to St Cuthbert's Church. She was frequently seen sitting on a wall in the churchyard, pointing sorrowfully at her stump. When the Palace was converted into the workhouse, she took pity on the inmates, and made them coffee. Moving without the sound of footsteps, only the rustle of her silky dress, she would summon the matron by banging on her door – presumably with her right hand – when anyone was taken ill. For some strange reason, legend has it that when she ventures outside her usual environment she turns into a white rabbit. In the 1830s a spooky bunny roamed nocturnally from Tubwell Row over to Priestgate. Parents locked their children inside for fear of them being tormented by the furry fiend. In the end shopkeeper George Rowell, who sold goods from somewhere between Bakehouse Hill and Church Row, owned up and admitted that the nightwalking rabbit was no ghost, but one that he owned. It covered a wide area, he said but always returned home before dawn. Mr Rowell was found dead in his shop one day in 1841, but the rabbit was not implicated. People often referred to Lady Jarratt as Lady Charity, presumbly because of her kindness towards the inmates of the workhouse, but to one poor pedlar she was anything but charita-ble. He ran a pitiful shop in the Leadyard and on a Monday rented a stall in the market but such was the paucity of his stock that it couldn't be in two places at once. So when he opened up his stall he had to close his shop and remove all his goods to the market. Sadly the poor man could not afford any means of conventional conveyance, so he had to rely on the borrowed muscle power of young boys. Late one night after a hard day's trading, the boys were heavily laden returning his unsold items to the shop. Suddenly this white face popped up from behind a wall, and appeared to be about to speak. The boys were dumbstruck, until their leader shouted 'Lady Jarrett, Lady Jarrett'. As one, they dropped all the goods and turned on their heels and fled. For the poor man the ghost's appearance spelled ruin. Everything he owned lay broken in the gutter.

This was one of the last reported sightings of Lady Jarratt although she did have another trick up her remaining sleeve. In 1870 the Palace was sold to Richard Luck for £2,000. In a letter he told how when he started demolition work, the ghost appeared to him.

'The end room was where Lady Jarrett was murdered and the bloodstains which could not be washed off were there. I was soon very much engaged in my work when I heard footsteps coming out of this room and I could feel it was her Ladyship. I could hear the rustle of her silk dress and she came close until I could feel her breath and her dress as she stooped over my shoulder to see what I was doing. I stood it for a very short while and then bolted along the corridor as hard as I could go.'

In 1938, Darlington Corporation removed the last remains of the old palace, and Lady Jarratt has never been known to walk again although there are rumours that her silky swish has been heard along the distant corridors of the Town Hall.

The Sad Story of Cicely Kirby

A book, a play and a musical have been written based on the myth of Cicely Kirby and so now it is difficult to say what is fact and what is poetic licence. The young domestic servant Cicely was murdered in 1745 in Blackwell Lane by a soldier called Sam Addy, one of the King's troops stationed in Darlington. On the night of the Battle of Culloden Addy and Cicely's real lover, Jack Langstaffe, lay wounded side by side on the field. Pain prevented them from sleeping and their thoughts strayed to the past as men will 'if the great mystery seems near at hand'. But then, according to Dr Manson who wrote a book on

Cicely, they were startled back to the present when in front of their very eyes 'a greenish light began to suffuse itself into the tent and they both saw standing before them Cicely Kirby. The features were visible in the light that seemed to exhale from them and to flicker around the whole form of the girl. For a few seconds it stood there and then, raising its hands as in entreaty, slowly disappeared from sight without appearing to move from the spot where it stood.' Addy shrieked: 'O Cicely!' and lost consciousness, but the following morning, when he knew death was close at hand, he confessed that he had killed the girl.

To his horror Langstaffe revealed through his pain that Cicely had been his lover. 'But I thought Trothie was her lover, and I have always hated him,' said Addy before recounting the whole sorry story. 'We were at a town called Darnton last autumn. I saw Trothie with that girl and thought they were sweethearts. Then one morning I met her in a lane between Darnton and a place called Blackwell. There was nobody about and to vex him and her I stopped her. She was plucky and in a struggle between us she fell, and striking her head against a tree root, lay stunned. She seemed dead at first, but when I saw she was breathing I thought I would prevent her telling any tales to Trothie and would revenge myself on him too by killing her out.'

As Addy told how he strangled her with his handkerchief and hid her poor body in the bushes, his mouth filled with blood. Turning his murderer's face towards the rising sun, he died. Broken-hearted Langstaffe soon followed him, hopefully to be reunited with Cicely. But, curiouser and curiouser, in 1853, a century after Cicely's sad demise, workmen digging up a hedge in Blackwell Lane unearthed the skeleton of a young woman. She had been buried doubled up, and clothes and even shoes were still clinging to her remains. Her teeth were said to be perfect. It is believed that the men reburied the body.

Early this century a rumour sprang up in the Blackwell area that a stone without inscription on the side of the road was the spot where a soldier had murdered his sweetheart. According to the legend of the time, animals had always scratched at the area, and if the path was ever recoated with ashes there would always be a hole there next morning. Then, in 1935, roadworker Walter Wake was employed widening the road near new houses. His operations caused him to dig up the ancient footpath, and his spade uncovered what looked like a turnip. He looked again, and realised it was a bone. Soon he had uncovered a whole skeleton. It is believed that the bones were reburied, perhaps for the third time, and the road built over the top.

The Ghost Of North Road Station

More than 100 years ago, somewhere in the cellars beneath North Road station, a porter committed suicide. His ghost has appeared many times over the years, walking along the platform towards the iron staircase, with a dog at his heels. Never, though, has he had such an impact as on his first appearance in the 1850s. At that time the Stockton to Darlington line crossed the Great North Road at a level crossing as the bridge had not been built. The nightwatchmen had a little cabin next to the crossing and one winter's night, at about midnight, James Durham started his rounds. He went for his supper in a cellar under the platform that was once part of the railwayman's cottage and still had a fireplace and a gas lamp. He turned up the gas, sat down on a bench and opened his bait tin. Then he spotted an unearthly intrusion – an apparition smartly dressed in a cut-away coat with gilt buttons, a turned up collar and a Scotch cap. At its heels was a large black retriever dog. The ghost walked nonchantly towards the fire, but suddenly raised a fist and struck James a powerful blow to the body which caused a strange sensation. James jumped up, and mustering all his strength, delivered the ghost a powerful right jab. His punch went clean through his assailant's body and hit the fireplace, severely bruising his knuckles. But the ghost was hurt. It shrieked and reeled backwards against the wall, whereupon the snarling retriever grabbed James' leg and bit him. Although a medical examination later found no teethmarks, James was convinced he felt pain. Obviously the ghost knew when it was onto a loser. It regained its balance and composure, clicked its tongue at the hound, and the uneasy pair retreated into the coal cellar. James followed with a lantern, but although there was no other way out he could see no sign of the fighting spook.

When the story of the punch-up entered public gossip there was much talk in town and it became known that a railway clerk called Winter, who kept a black dog and dressed exactly as described, had shot himself in the station office. His body had been placed in the porters' cellar for a time. Edward Pease and James' local vicar all testified to his reliability and said he was a teetotaller who slept during the day so he could perform his night job to the best of his abilities. The Society for Psychical Research investigated the claims and in 1891 published a Census of Hallucinations in a magazine edited by The Northern Echo's then editor W.T. Stead. The story of the brawling ghost was one of the most thrilling anecdotes. A James Durham died on January 9 1917, aged 75, and was buried in North Cemetery. Almost exactly one hundred years later, before North Road station was taken out of operation, the ghost made a return journey. It was a snowy day in the Fifties. The ticket collector swore he heard a train pull in. The carriage door opened, someone got out, slammed the door shut, and the train pulled away. The person was then heard to walk across the platform. The ticket collector naturally expected the passenger to pass by his booth, but after a few minutes no-one came. He looked out, but the station was deserted, and the snow on the platform lay untouched and virginal.

These are only two of many reported hauntings made by the railway ghost. In the early Eighties a group of train buffs, including Councillor Barrie Lamb who went on to become Mayor in 1989-90, slept over in the station which had by this time been converted into a museum to mount a night-long vigil guarding valuable exhibits on loan. All of the party of rail-lovers slept soundly and undisturbed, but when they awoke next morning a small puddle of water had mysteriously formed on the platform. The question on their lips was had the ghostly porter's dog spent a penny during the night?

The Hauntings Of Harewood

The Harewood Hill area of Darlington is said to be the most be-spooked part of town. It is chiefly noted for headless gentlemen who disappear in flames, headless ladies, white cats, white rabbits, white dogs, 'shapes that walk at the dead of night, and clank their chains', and the infamous devil dog. In the past, the area was called the Glassensikes. The name derives from the ancient word 'glassene', meaning blue or grey, with 'sike', an old legal term for any stream less than a beck, added. One bewitching moonlit midnight, an old gentleman, said to be a very reliable source, was returning on foot from Oxen-le-Field. When he reached Harewood Hill he was amazed to see the head of a large animal appear from behind a stile. The black head was followed by a black body, the size of which he had never seen before, and then a black tail, the length of which no-one had ever seen before. The hound leapt into the road, and there it stood, staring straight at him.

This hound of the Glassensikes didn't flinch, its gaze probing deep into his soul. Fearlessly, he clicked his fingers to attract its attention. But it was no good. The brute was immoveable, and stared ferociously

The Hound of the Glassensikes

upon him. The gent had had enough. The purpose of his journey had been to explode the myth of the Glassensikes spooks, but he had failed. In panic he turned and fled, now of the confirmed opinion that strange spirits did indeed roam this part of town.

The headless man who vanished into a ball of fire was another favourite Harewood apparition. He apparently lived in a boggy field near the Glassensikes and on one celebrated night 'a woeful wight was unable to return from Blackwell in consequence of a great gulph of fire'. However, the burning man – no doubt a close relative of Will O' the Wisp – has not been seen since the Harewood Hill houses were built and the field improved and built upon. Similarly, the hound of hell has been driven away by the increased traffic along Grange Road.

Another headless ghost who, sadly, no longer enjoys public appearances haunted Prescott's stile, which was on a footpath from Harewood to Blackwell. The stile was named after the Prescott family who lived in a mansion at Blackwell. Whether this poor man is a relative of the Prescott family is unclear, but certainly the family seems to have an uncannily close connection with restless spirits. Their Blackwell mansion was said to be haunted by Old Pinkney who wandered around wearing a red nightcap. The mansion was served by a well underneath it known as 'Pink-e-ney's well', but it was never tapped for water after nightfall.

Yet another spooking in Harewood Grove concerns a ghost who wears silk. It inhabits a house in the road and has a lot of unusual habits. Sounds of breaking sticks and chairs being dragged over the floor are often heard. Then the ghost emerges from underneath a bed.

It reveals itself to have half a man's head then jumps into bed beside a person and pretends to be a child. Many people scoff at such reports calling them the result of a troubled mind, but a 19th Century historian wrote: 'It is true that these awful visions occassionally resolved themselves into a pony shackled in an adjoining field, or Stamper's white dog, or a pair of sweethearts under the cold moon, but still a vast amount of credible evidence exists about the fallen glories of the night-roaming ghost of Glassensikes.'

Why Harewood is such a popular place for ghosts is difficult to say, although residents of Weardale in past centuries would undoubtedly have said that it was because the inhabitants of the area were so stupid they believed anything. For some strange reason, the people of Weardale were of the opinion that the people of Harewood were a 'clan of ninnies'. They had a couple of favourite stories with which to illustrate this. The residents of Harewood were one day astonished to find a rare cuckoo had strayed into their midsts and so they clubbed together to build a wall of stones around the bird to keep it captive as it sat in a tree. Unfortunately a large dog – quite possibly the father of the hound of hell – turned up and started barking at the bird as it sat with amusement watching the labours of the natives. As the people of Harewood were so stupid, the story goes, they had omitted from their construction brief a roof for their edifice and so the cuckoo, when it tired of the dog, simply flew up and away. The residents blamed the dog and couldn't see the folly of their ways.

The other ninny-ish story harks back to the days when the first road to Harewood was completed. 'A surveyor drove up to inspect the new work. He was seated in a four-wheeled carriage, which was a fresh object of wonderment to the clan of ninnies. The whole population ran after it, declaring to each other: "Darra, lad, d'girt wheil's gaun t'owertak t'little un".' Whether the big one did succeed in overtaking the little one is not recorded.

The Barquest of Throstle-nest

In times long past in a glen between Darlington and Haughton-le-Skerne lived the Barquest. This creature inhabited Throstle-nest in the area which is now Haughton Road when it was a thickly-wooded area. Its howls would keep anyone in the area awake all night, and it became known as the 'roaring ghost'. Usually its howling preceeded some great calamity in the district. The name 'barquest' comes from the Danish meaning 'carriage for the dead' and the appearance of the barquest was a harbinger for the Grim Reaper. Its party trick was to accost luckless travellers. Like all good Darlington ghosts, it took on various forms including a beautiful maiden, a cat, and the inevitable large shaggy dog. Indeed, it became known as Padfoot due to the quiet, stealthy manner in which it approached its victims.

The Barquest has now sadly retired and the area it haunted has undergone substantial development in the last century. During building work many human bodies were discovered and these are believed to have been the victims of Scottish raiders.

The Lament of Laurel Cottage

Nearly 200 years ago the land between Stanhope Road and Bondgate was a plantation and in a small clearing in the middle there stood Laurel Cottage. The North Star newspaper of April 3, 1907 reports how about 50 years earlier a Darlington businessman and his wife were returning home at about midnight and as they crossed what is now Stanhope Green the gentleman looked behind him. He was startled to see the figure of an old woman in a long dress coming towards him. He was even more startled when the woman passed through a hedge without climbing over it. Being the perfect gentleman he did not want to alarm his dear wife, so he told her nothing, and carried on walking, only at a quicker pace. The couple were regular late night visitors to their friends in Greenbank Road and on the way home the gentleman often spotted the strange woman who did not need a gate, but he never told his wife.

Then one evening his terrified maid rushed into his house and fainted. She had been out courting, and her romantic activities had come to a sudden end when her boyfriend was chased out of Greenbank by the ghostly old woman. The story spread, and was corroborated by a Methodist preacher who had lived at Laurel Cottage for many years. He said when he prayed in his bedroom he experienced a spooky sensation of someone trying to place a shroud over him.

His niece had also been frightened by a woman wearing a coal-scuttle bonnet who, in the middle of the night, came out from behind the curtains and tried to kiss her as she slept. A month later he allowed his sister to sleep in the haunted room only to find her packing her bags and leaving the next morning. Sometime later the sister told him she had been approached by an old woman in a quaint bonnet who had tried to kiss her. The sister said: 'I would not have slept in that room again for all Darlington. But I did not want to tell you because I knew it would upset your wife.' The ghostly story was now gaining momentum and letters about it started appearing in the Darlington and Stockton Times. Eventually an acceptable explanation was settled upon. Laurel Cottage was a house of ill-repute kept by an old woman. A well-to-do pedlar used to stay there when he was in the district on business. One night the old woman murdered him to get her hands on his loot. When she died, such was the enormity of her crime that she was not allowed into the afterlife and so her spirit haunted the cottage and the nearby plantation. When Laurel Cottage was demolished to make way for Granville Terrace – now Woodland Road – builder John Hindle disturbed a compost heap in the plantation. Underneath he found a skeleton – presumably the remains of the old pedlar.

The Ghost In Room 11

The George Inn at Piercebridge is renowned throughout the world for its grandfather clock that stopped, never to go again, when its owner died. This story is widely regarded as a fallacy, but the tale of the ghost in Room 11 is one that has never been disproved. It is a sad, sad story that lies behind the uncanny appearance of a beautiful young girl dressed in white. She was the daughter of one the first landlords at the inn which highwayman Dick Turpin is reputed to have used as a hide-out.

Tragically crossed in love, the heartbroken young lady is said to have hanged herself from a beam in Room 11. Now she appears rather eerily in the spring, but only if a young man is staying alone in the room. She is said to approach him gently and lay her hand tenderly on his shoulder – no doubt hoping it is her lover returned.

United in Silence

To tell this tale a vow of silence has to be broken. In the Fifties it was told to new employees who came to work at the United bus company offices in Grange Road, but always before it was recounted the uninitiated listener had to pledge secrecy. The United management wanted the whole business covered up so employees could get on with their work without fear of a haunting. The back of the premises was an ancient stately home or convent. United used the cellar for storing documents. At the end of each financial year all the out of date books were stacked in the fireplace for the caretaker to burn, but no-one would enter the cellar on their own, even with the lights on. A respected spinster explained this chilling tale to one new clerk:

'When the house was a large home of a monied-man, a maid

employed by the family was made pregnant by the owner of the house. The baby was born and to all intents and purposes it was totally normal, except that it had a birthmark which proved without a shadow of doubt that the master of the house was the father. So, at the dead night, the master took the newborn babe to the cellar and burnt it in the fireplace. The following morning, the poor mother committed suicide.' Since that day the ghost of a young woman in servant's clothes is reported to have been seen walking along the corridor, wringing her hands, as if she were looking for something. The immediate thought would be that her condition was the advanced stages of waiting for a bus if it wasn't for the fact that her spooky stroll always terminated at the fireplace.

Lurking In the Lane

Until 1870 the main road between Cockerton and Darlington was a narrow, dirty bridle-track with dense, spooky plantations on either side. Travellers feared to go there after sunset because not only was it frequented by undesireable characters, but there was also a disturbingly large number of ghosts flitting about the darkness. In 1860 a gas main was laid down the lane – now Woodland Road – and people were so perturbed by the number of unearthly shadows in that part of town that they demanded with a huge petition that the maximum number of lamps be provided to protect them from robbers and ghosts. But they had good cause to worry about extraterrestial beings lurking in the lane for the lonely stretch of road had a grim history of violent tragedies.

Going as far back as 1242, the time of Henry III, a traveller named Thomas Broadhead, who was quietly minding his own business, was brutally murdered by a pauper called Allan Halkerbain. Almost two centuries later, after years of reported sightings of Thomas still strangely alive, a second aggressive episode occured which frightened the locals. A young solider tired of his unhappy life in the army hanged himself from a tree near where Holy Trinity Church is now. The soldier's ghost was added to a long catalogue of half-seen shapes and semi-heard noises said to emanate from the unlit depths of Woodland Road. These mysterious movements and spooky sounds were only dispelled by the advent of the gas lamp.

The Northern Echo

READER OFFER

The Northern Echo

COUNTY DURHAM TANKARD

—ONLY—
£10.95

The Northern Echo County Durham Tankard is beautifully crafted in fine quality pewter. It is engraved with five of Durham's best known attractions, all of which are renowned for their outstanding beauty - Raby Castle, Killhope Wheel, High Force, Bowes Museum and, of course, Durham Cathedral. Also featured is the world famous Locomotion No. 1 steam engine. *This super piece is worthy of personal collection or perfect as a gift.*

ORDER FORM

The Northen Echo County Durham Tankard is available now from the following Northern Echo offices.

Priestgate, Darlington, Newgate Street, Bishop Auckland, Saddler Street, Durham, High Street, Northallerton.

Alternatively, you can order by post by completing the form below and sending it to:

County Durham Tankard Offer, Promotons Dept., The Northern Echo, Priestgate, Darlington DL1 1NF.

Please send me:

_____ x County Durham Tankards @ £10.95
plus £1.50 per tankard postage & packing

I eclose a cheque / postal order for £_____
made payable to 'North of England Newspapers.

Name...
Address ....
....
Post code ....Telephone ....

29-001

118

Index

Index

Bibliography

The History and Antiquities of the Parish of Darlington, in the Bishoprick by W Hylton Dyer Longstaffe, 1854
The Book of Darlington by George Flynn, 1987
Rural Darlington, Farm, Mansion and Suburb by Vera Chapman, 1977
Darlington Memoirs by E. Mountford, unpublished (Darlington Centre for Local Studies)
The Robert Scarr Cuttings Books (Darlington Centre for Local Studies)
Archives from The Northern Echo, Darlington and Stockton Times, Northern (Evening) Despatch